DEDICATION

For those of us who are faced with a challenge, may the good Lord always help us to understand its true purpose.

ACKNOWLEDGEMENTS

To my father and mother, Dave and Char Meek: I know how hard it was for you both to relive that horrific experience. But over 20 years later you both stepped up to the challenge without hesitation.

To my sister, Wendi DeYoung: Even with a newborn daughter, you somehow managed to find the time to show the world what an aspiring author you are. I pray that you use this as a jumping off point to help launch your own writing career. You always have my full support and encouragement.

To my wife and lifelong friend, Christine Meek: There is just so much to be said, but words just aren't enough. Thank you for being my friend, my inspiration, my challenge, and so many times my reason for getting up in the morning.

I love you all.

Contents

From the ER to the Stars

From the ER to the Stars

vi

Preface

 The effects of trauma do not affect just the victim.
It affects all the people around that person. I don't think I
really understood this to be true until more than 20 years
after my accident when I was out on a "guy's weekend"
with my dad. I knew my story from my point of view, but
I got to hear my dad's story for the first time when he was
talking to a stranger at the bar. As my dad was sharing the
story of the accident, he reached in his pocket and pulled
out the little date book from 1989 that he carried every day
since the accident. On that fateful day, his life changed
forever, not just mine. He held on to those memories, not
just in his head, but he kept those memories written down
next to his heart.

 We all have a story. You have a story. You have
gone through or are going through tough challenges. But
those challenges do not just affect you. Your recovery
isn't all for you. Those that love you, those that care for
you are affected as well. It is a tough time for everyone.
All the people in your life learn new coping skills, learn
new conversations, and learn how to heal. Those around
you hurt for you and feel helpless when they can't take the
pain away from you. You need to learn to heal together.

 This book was written because the story needed to
be told. In 20 years, my dad and I had never really talked
about the accident. I never knew how it affected him or
my mom and sister, and I never thought that it affected my
wife since she entered my life well after the accident. But it
did and it still does. The writing of this book started a
conversation and led to the healing of old wounds—not
just mine, but my entire family's. This is a book made of 5

stories: mine, my mom's, my dad's, my sister's, and my wife's. .I pray that this book can help start conversations for you and those you love. I selfishly hope that my story of how I succeeded in overcoming my tragedy brings you hope in your struggle. In that way, my accident had purpose and meaning. That's what we all look for in life: the meaning of it all.

TIME LINE:

1971
>   – Born

1987 – 1988
>   – 3rd Year of High School in Florida (Florida Air Academy)

September 1988 – December 1988
>   – 4th Year of High School in Melbourne, FL

January 1989 – April 1989
>   – 4th Year of High School in Hudsonville, MI

April 4, 1989
>   – The Accident

June 1989
>   – High School Graduation Ceremony

August 1989
>   – Received High School Diploma

September 1989
>   – Community College in Grand Rapids, MI

1990 – 1991
>   – Embry-Riddle Aeronautical University Daytona, FL

1991 – 1992
>   – Community College in Grand Rapids, MI

1993 – 1995
>   – Central Michigan University

1994
>   – Met Christine Woolsey

1996
>   – Married Christine

1996 – 1998
>   – Embry-Riddle Prescott, AZ

1998
>   – Graduated with a Bachelor of Science in Electrical Engineering

From the ER to the Stars

1999

    – Taran Edward Meek (First son) born

2000

    – Hunter Keith Meek (Second Son) born

2007

    – Graduated with a Master's Degree in Aeronautical Science

2013

    – Went to work with NASA Independent Verification and Validation (NASA IV&V) to perform software verification for human space flight.

CHAPTER 1

Proverbs 3:5-6 – Trust in the LORD with all your heart, and do not lean on your own understanding. In all your ways acknowledge Him, and He will make straight your paths.

In the small, rural town of Jamestown, Michigan, surrounded by nothing more than hills, fields of unkempt grass and corn—lots and lots of corn—I lived with my parents and younger sister. Our A-framed house looked more like a Swiss chalet than the typical ranch house you would expect to see in western Michigan. Cows and chickens were part of the landscape seen from our deck. The smells of farmland filled my nose and the lowing of cows lulled me to sleep. I lived out in the middle of nowhere, but it was my home.

As far as neighbors went, there was only one or two large farm houses other than my family's, and the only landmark was the intersection of two country roads surrounded by fields of overgrown grass. Western Michigan is very hilly, and the point where the two roads met was no exception. Neither of the roads were ever very busy, and as far as corners go, this intersection wasn't anything spectacular.

The intersection was only about a quarter of a mile from my house. The road I lived on was 24th Avenue, while the intersecting road was Byron Road. The city designers decided, seemingly randomly, that Byron Road was the busier of the two roads. So 24th Avenue had the stop signs, but Byron Road did not.

Byron Road was hilly, and I remember riding my bike

1

and having to start hitting the brakes long before actually coming to 24th Avenue. The summit of the hill was to the east which created a blind spot, and when the sun was setting, another blind spot was created to the west.

The speed limit on Byron Road was 55 miles per hour at the time. But it was out in the middle of nowhere, so most of the time, people going over those hills were going much faster than the speed limit. To be safe, travelers on 24th Avenue needed to cross Byron Road before a truck or car came flying over that hill. And on the evening of April 4, 1989, I wasn't so lucky trying to cross Byron Road.

I had borrowed my dad's small two-door pickup truck so that I could drive myself to work in Holland, Michigan. The sun was setting, and it was a beautiful spring evening. My mind was on the movies playing at the theater where I worked. I was thinking about school, tests, and girls. That is when I got caught in the gauntlet of blind spots and never saw the other car coming over that hill.

Almost instantaneously, there came the crash of metal, the sound of glass breaking, and the smell of gasoline and burning rubber. When the sound of screeching brakes subsided, absolute silence followed.

I had stopped at that two-way stop on 24th Avenue, and I was proceeding across that same intersection just like I had done so many times in the past. It might have been the sun setting. It could have also been some distraction. Then again, it might have been the fact that I couldn't see what was coming over the hill. But some combination of these factors, or possibly divine intervention, caused me to pull out into that intersection at the precise time that put me into the path of another vehicle. I will probably never know the exact reasons but, based on everything I have been through, I choose to believe that it was divine intervention that caused the accident.

No matter what the reasoning, against all odds, I eventually woke up. I would have never planned for this to happen. But this may have been exactly what I needed.

The moment just before an accident is the point where many people know it's about to happen. I had no idea that the truck that impacted me was en route as I made my way across Byron Road. I can discern this because of the blast pattern of the safety glass that exploded toward my head as the door was impacted. I was facing forward at the time, so although there were countless lacerations along the side of my face and although my ear was left dangling nearly ripped off, my eyes were both spared the carnage.

I heard later that the accident was technically considered my fault. I am not sure this was true as I never got a ticket for it, but I was surprised to hear that I could have been slapped with a "failure to control a vehicle" conclusion by the local authorities. In my mind, I liken it to a failure to control a vehicle sliding on a patch of ice or being unable to control a vehicle as it was being thrown 100 feet from the point of impact. Either way, I never got a ticket.

The instantaneous results of the accident were horrific. The other truck had come over the hill to the east and impacted my driver's side door, leaving my truck in three pieces about 100 feet down the road. The cab of my truck was mangled and covered with blood, my blood. I do not remember anything about this gruesome scene, but this is what I have been able to recreate based on the evidence and few pictures I have found after the accident.

The cab of my dad's truck was crushed, cocooning my body within. Thankfully, the first responders were skilled with the "Jaws of Life" and were able extract what was left of me without severing my spinal cord. Because of their heroic actions, I "walked away" from that accident with minimal physical defects.

Due to the absolute desolation reported by the Good Samaritan that called in about my accident, a medical helicopter was dispatched to my location. It was many years later that by chance, or another instance of divine intervention, my mom met a member of the crew from that flight and confirmed our worst fears of what had happened. When the helicopter arrived at the scene of the accident, the first responders radioed in a "DOA," which stands for Dead on Arrival. This meant that the victim was not expected to survive the flight back to the hospital. The crew member that talked to my mom also gave her the pictures included with this book. He told my mom that my heart had stopped somewhere along the flight. But it wasn't my time yet. God had other plans for me.

A police officer dispatched to tell my parents of the plight of their only son, answered their worried questions with a simple, "We just need you to get to the hospital right away." There was no hope offered from those in uniform.

Once my parents got to the hospital, hope was once again elusive. The doctors were occupied with desperately trying to save my life. This meant that my parents were left in the hands of a crisis counselor. According to my mom, the consoling method they employed were simple statements such as, "He's alive for now," but they "didn't have any further information." My distraught parents were shuffled into a small isolated waiting room until developments with my condition were deemed to be releasable to the family. In effect, they were told, "Wait here and keep praying. We will let you know when we can." Minutes turned into hours.

This continued until my condition became more stable and the hospital was able to release further updates. Gradually, statements like, "It's a critical time right now. We aren't sure that he is going to make it," were slowly replaced with less dramatic statements such as, "He is stable, but we aren't sure how much comprehension you will be able to expect. This sort of thing is not an exact science. It just takes time to assess the full extent of the traumatic head injuries."

It was many days before I was coherent enough for my memory to return. I was not aware what my parents were being told, but once I was on that road to recovery, I too was spoon-fed the same sort of feedback. Pieces of information about my condition were fed to me a little at a time by the many doctors and nurses who treated me over the many weeks and months to come. I have never held this myopic insight against them. Really. Based on how many developments took place since my accident, I can understand why medicine is not an exact science. There are so many variables at play that you can't predict the future. Some things are beyond our control. Some things are beyond our comprehension. It takes the One who can see the maze from all angles to interpret the variables and set the right controls.

CHAPTER 2

Ephesians 5:15-16 – Be very careful, then, how you live – not as unwise but as wise, making the most of every opportunity, because the days are filled with evil.

At this point, I would like to take a step back. As mentioned, prior to my accident, I was headed down a particular path in the maze of life. I had a very specific direction. It might not have been exactly the right direction, but my life had a purpose and a direction up to that point.

I grew up in a small rural community. When I say "rural," I mean that there were almost 200 people, so there was never a busy season. I lived with my parents and my sister out on a farm in the country. This property could be considered a farm in the loosest sense of the word. We had horses at one point in time. Chickens grazed sporadically. Both of my parents worked elsewhere, so there was little time to grow plants other than a bed of weeds that helped to hide a tomato plant or two. The fields around us were filled with cows. You could sling-shot a rock in any direction without fear of hitting a single shack. Corn was the main crop. Fields of corn could be seen for miles. If you have seen the movie "Footloose" with Kevin Bacon, then you have a pretty good analogy of my life prior to my accident.

Our family had relocated to this microcosm many years earlier. Despite that, I never felt accepted or included. Kids picked on me because I was skinny, had asthma, and didn't enjoy sports. It is only a guess, but I would say that the teachers rejected me because I liked to ask questions. I have always been curious. Admittedly, I just didn't like answers that didn't make any sense to me. I always wanted more of an explanation. So even though I grew up in this rural environment, I remained an outsider. As I grew up, I turned into a rebellious teenager in the eyes of some. But honestly, I was more bored than rebellious.

High school was difficult—not academically, unless you count trying to stay awake, but rather socially. I thought a lot about just leaving and going to some faraway place. I became enlightened in the art of creative attendance until that caught up with me. During my sophomore year of high school, I was inadvertently blessed with a way out. I managed to catch mononucleosis, also known as mono or the kissing disease. It almost sounds romantic, but trust me, it isn't. Since then, I have always had to tell myself to be careful what I wish for.

Mono caused me to miss a lot of school my sophomore year. Of course, I wasn't missing it at all. On a particularly overcast day, during a particularly overcast winter, I was pushed to the edge. I got a call from the school politely informing me that I was approaching the limit of allowable absences. This pushed me over the edge. I realized I had to make a choice right then and there. I told them to please take me off their calling list as I didn't care for their product. So, midway through my sophomore year of high school, I decided to pursue other opportunities.

In other words, I dropped out.

Needless to say, after I quit school, I was a teen searching for mischief. Whereas school was boring, my new freedom brought possibility and excitement. Now I had time to follow new pursuits. The world was my oyster, and I was feeling a little shellfish. One thing I did was invoke my inner engineer: I re-designed my windshield washing system in my car to create an automotive water cannon that connected to a tank under my hood. While driving by pedestrians off to the side of the road, I could spray the victims with water to watch how they reacted. Of course, they reacted by sending the police to my door.

As yet inexperienced with having police at the door, Mom complained to Dad when he arrived home from a full shift at work. Teenagers have a habit of not listening. Dad insisted I sit down to a meeting before dinner. His concern started with, "What do you want to do? ... blah ... blah ... blah ... Where do you want to go with your life? ... blah ... blah ... We need to set out a plan because you are smart. And you're upsetting your mother ... blah ... constructive with your talents ... blah ... so what do you want to do WHEN you graduate from high school?"

There was no "IF" in my parent's vocabulary when it came to high school graduation. You see, my mom never finished high school herself. And although dad never attended college, both my parents insisted that I finish high school. My parents were hard workers who were raised by hard working families. There was no question about graduation from high school for me, but there were no expectations beyond that.

When my dad asked about a plan for my life, I gave him the best answer I could think of. I was looking for a way to expand my horizons and deliver myself from what was constraining me. I answered, "I want to fly." Easy. The simple answer wasn't only a daydream. My entire being wanted to be sky high and to fly from this place where our family settled. I had hopes of finally finding that faraway place that I had only dreamed about.

Flying gave me a goal in life. In the days before the internet, this meant extensive research at libraries all around the area. My parents and I checked out Air Force boarding schools where I would be able to pursue my dream to the best of my abilities. At the time, there were two Air Force boarding schools to choose from. There was one in Virginia and another in Florida. It was no contest for me. Florida meant sun, sand, ocean, and an opportunity to live on the space coast. The seed was planted.

At this point in my life, I felt as though I was drifting. It was almost like a haphazard walk through the maze, taking whatever path seemed to look like the most fun at the time. Looking back on this period though, I see something much different. Seemingly unrelated events were somehow pointing in a direction I would have never been able to understand at the time.

For instance, I have always had difficulties with school, because I wasn't being challenged. Because of this, I would come up with creative ways of entertaining myself. In those days, there was no "homeschooling" option. There were also no online courses that you could take. The most interesting option available to me was the "Co-Op" option. This was where you could go to a normal half day of school and then do the other half day taking vocational classes. This was where you would learn a trade like industrial electronics, plumbing, or sheep shearing. However, this wasn't an option for me until my 3rd year of high school. I ended up quitting when I was in my 2nd year.

Undoubtedly, had I stayed one more year, I would have enrolled just to be out of school for the half day. But I can tell you now that I would have hated the career I would have ended up with. Without catching mono, I would have taken the path of least resistance and stayed in school. Mononucleosis is one of the indicators for me now that leads me to believe that God might have been trying to lead me even back then.

After I left school, I had fun for a while, but days grew monotonous. Tension built between me and my parents as I battled with their expectations of me graduating from high school. I really wasn't opposed to this. In fact, I had every intention to go back to school the following year. It was just so boring, and I was looking for every excuse to do something different.

When my parents gave me the "option" of going to

school in Florida, it was a no-brainer. I am sure God's involvement was probably to force my parents to make the decision that they did with military school. Although, this might have been an easy decision for them to make given that I was nailing innocent joggers with my car water cannon. But more to the point, I was forced to make a decision. I could have fought my parents on the decision to send me to military school. I am also sure they would have given me another chance. But I knew I needed something else, and I truly wanted to be good. I just needed a way out.

From the ER to the Stars

CHAPTER 3

Jeremiah 29:7 – Also seek the peace and prosperity of the city to which I have carried you into exile. Pray to the Lord for it, because if it prospers, you too will prosper.

Florida Air Academy in Melbourne, Florida, welcomed me in the summer of 1987, and I quickly learned that I was not allowed to leave the school campus. So at 16 years old, my dreams of sun, sand, and ocean in that faraway place became as vaporous as an early morning fog. It was a devastating reality for me. After months of planning and anticipation, I had come all that way only to see all my hopes and aspirations fade away.

At this point, I was forced to make a huge decision. I had been fighting the system my whole life. My natural reaction to any confrontation with authority was to provide the collective administration with whatever snide comment I could muster up. But this wasn't the path I wanted to take. I was truly sorry for putting my parents through what I had forced them to endure. I wanted to change.

More than that, my new school had a strict no tolerance policy. They were strict and had limited patience. They could send a rebellious student home without returning the tuition costs. To me, this seemed like an all-too-real temptation for a big institution. I knew that my parents could barely afford my rehabilitation, and it would not be fair for them to lose that money on account of my behavior. So I decided to curb my temptation for rebellion. I decided that if I had any hope of succeeding, I should try to work within the system. With an honest desire to reform and make the best of my situation, I decided to try and make myself useful.

Moving-in-day was pure chaos. Kids meandered around and parents asked for directions. Noise and confusion abounded. As I wandered around trying to find my own place in this mess, I saw a whiteboard with a written message that they were looking for someone to be a "Canteen OIC." I had absolutely no idea what a Canteen OIC was, and I did something very out of character for me at the time. I went up to the highest-ranking student in the building and asked, "Excuse me, sir, could you tell me what a Canteen OIC is?" I had every notion of replying to whatever answer he gave me with, "Oh, I see."

As it turned out, he was the one that had written the message. He told me that he was looking for a Canteen Officer in Charge. I still had no idea what this was, but it had the word officer in it, so I figured it couldn't be all that bad. I almost gave him my original response, but changed my mind at the last minute. Instead, I said, "Oh, you mean me?"

He asked, "Did the Commandant send you to see me?"

I said, "No, but I am a top-notch officer variety. So you must be looking for me." I wish I had a camera at that moment. The look in his eyes was a combination of surprise, disgust, and awe.

He said something along the lines of, "Boy, you have a set of brass cojones. I guess you will do just fine."

Once again, I must talk about divine guidance. So how exactly was God involved in this transaction? This was a prime example of me acting somewhat out of character. Aside from being a little on the cocky side, I was socially awkward. I didn't like making waves—particularly when I might get caught in the waves. This was especially valid when coming into a new environment like I was. So why did I speak up the way I did? Looking back on this memory, the answer is simple. I was out of my element, and I knew it. I asked for some guidance. Like I had said, I truly wanted to be good.

My help came in the form of speaking up at just the right time and with just the right implication to put me directly where I needed to be. This was me following what my heart was telling me to do. At the time, I didn't exactly know why this was a good idea. I just went with it. I was on autopilot. But I can say that it worked. This provided me, unknowingly, with the haven I desperately needed.

The Canteen was a little student-run store located outside in a patio area. During their free time, the kids could go out there to eat a snack, smoke, and hang out. The canteen had set hours when it was open. But it did most of its business right before class in the morning and between the hours after dinner and "lights out" or bedtime. Students could use their $10 a week allowance to buy some candy, soda, or they could just come and hang out with friends. There were stone tables that opened out to the soccer field behind the school. There were generally a good number of students, and many of these were smokers. So aside from giving the place an old cigarette smell, this ensured that there was always a little mess to clean.

My job as the Canteen Officer in Charge or Canteen OIC was to manage a group of students who served as a military style cleaning crew. These "volunteers" were usually not volunteers at all. When a student did something wrong or made some sort of infraction, they were assigned a number of "hours" that they had to work off in order to pay penance for their crime. Being the Canteen OIC, I got to pick and manage which volunteers got to help me out. Ensuring that the Canteen was spotless meant cleaning it a couple times a day.

The job itself didn't pay anything, literally. But it showed my captors that I was willing to take on responsibility, and it gave me a place to escape to. In the Canteen, I could come and go at my leisure. Because the Canteen was my responsibility, there was always a reason for me to be there. Even if that reason was solely because I didn't want to stand in a group formation somewhere else.

What I enjoyed the most was coming out early just before sunrise. It was then that I could sit at one of those stone tables and watch the egrets out on the soccer field dancing around and poking through the marshy grass. In the mornings, there was always a light radiation fog (the technical term I learned from my weather class). So when the sun started to rise, you could watch the fog dissipate as the shadows moved across the field. Another reward was at night. This was because I was allowed to stay out after everyone else was in bed just to be sure that the Canteen was clean for the next day. Usually, by the time I leisurely made my way back to bed, all of the day's formations were done and I could slip into my room un-harassed by the authority.

Life at the Florida Air Academy was hard. The school was run by mostly retired military personnel. The staff that worked there consisted of all men in those days. This was probably because it was an all-male school. I had never been exposed to anyone who was in the military prior to this, so I was intrigued by the culture. I learned that the military style drills were monotonous, and the academics were more than a little challenging. This new-found challenge did a couple of things that really helped me cope with my new situation.

In my previous life, there were only a handful of times I actually sat down and spent any time doing my homework assignments. Most of the time, I got by with just memorizing the needed information right before a test and forgetting it shortly afterward. I also spent a lot of time trying to figure out the "minimal" effort to eke out a "C" that would keep me on the road to graduation. All in all, it wasn't a whole lot of fun. The classes all consisted of the basic math, English, and the most rudimentary science classes. Although I sometimes enjoyed some of the science classes, I really didn't enjoy English, and I could never quite grasp the point of the math classes that I was forced to take. I constantly felt like I was being forced through the meat grinder. Increasingly, I felt that after high school there wouldn't be anything left of me other than a big pile of hamburger.

In this military school, however, there was a two-hour block of time each night that was considered "study time." We were all forced to sit in our rooms at our desks and there was no talking allowed. This situation didn't force us to study, but what else was there to do for two hours while sitting at a desk without the ability to talk to anyone? And yes, the classes were more challenging. I was still forced to take the same sort of math and English classes, but in military school, I was part of the science club. So I really got to see some of the more practical applications of science. For instance, did you know that there are certain types of metal that are quite reactive when introduced to water? In fact, my professor showed us that when you throw a stick of potassium in the local stream it makes a six-foot water spout. Now that is applied science!

Along with all this, the military school accounted for every hour. So when you weren't in class, you were standing in formations, practicing military drills, waiting in lines for food, and the list goes on and on. During a handful of special occasions, we also got some limited free time. Yes, it was more challenging, but there was also less time to waste when you weren't being challenged.

This was also the first time I had lived away from my parent's house, and I felt isolated and alone. The Canteen became a much-needed escape for me.

Let's face it, change is hard. Adapting is even harder. I was isolated from the world in a place completely foreign to me. I was also submersed in a foreign culture, because I had never been exposed to military lifestyle or regiment.

My escape was the Canteen. But it was more than that. It was my catalyst. I spent a lot of my free time out at the Canteen since that was my charge. This was important to me for a couple of different reasons. The first reason was because it really forced me out of my comfort zone for the first time in my life. Prior to this, I would have been described as a loner. I felt out of place in crowds larger than three people, but overseeing the primary location for social gathering at the school forced me to adapt. It wasn't what I wanted, but looking back, I believe it is what I needed. Somewhere along the way, I found out that, in general, people aren't that bad. In fact, I found quite a few friends. I had to leave my comfort zone to figure this out and I have never looked back.

Spending my free time at the Canteen also helped me because I got to hear some pretty good "war stories." I call these war stories, because these stories were often barely within the limits of being believable. Some even fell outside the limits of being believable, but I found the stories really fascinating. Although I was in isolation compared to my prior life, my view of the world was expanding. Listening to these stories gave me my own dreams. I dreamt of traveling the world someday.

This was my new life. It was hard, but sometimes it was extremely rewarding. Aside from the Canteen, what really made military school fun was that I got to go out to the airport a couple of times a week for flying lessons. This meant I got to miss some school the legal way. I could adjust my flying lessons to accommodate the classes that I really didn't find very challenging or useful. Even though I was seldom able to leave the campus, I managed to build a world around myself. Every cloud does have a silver lining which. I got to see firsthand when I went flying.

There was only one weekend that I made it to the beach that first summer. By chance, or more than likely by divine intervention, the one time I did get away I met a cute blonde surfer girl named Rachel. We dated the whole summer. Of course, our dating consisted of phone conversations and brief meetings where we met each other on opposite sides of the fence.

Because school was challenging, I managed to keep myself from getting in any trouble. I made a number of friends over the course of the summer and I was happy. I also managed to accumulate enough credits in eight weeks to make up for missing my sophomore year. When it came time to sign up for the next full year, I was all over the opportunity. Rachel had to do very little to convince me that this was the high school I might want to attend for my junior year.

During my third year of high school, Rachel and I continued to grow our relationship. We got so serious that her family offered to take me in a couple of weekends a month to help me escape my military school sentence. Rachel lived with her grandma Margaret, her aunt Patricia, and her cousin Alex in a small house in the suburbs of Melbourne. Her family made me feel like I was back at home. They were my home away from home. It was more than I had dared to ask for. But all things must eventually come to an end.

When the school year ended, I didn't have the choice to go back to Florida Air Academy. Although my parent's income was in the middle-class category and they had plenty of love for their son who was starting to blossom, they didn't have the extra money to pay the Florida Air Academy tuition. Without the financial backing of my parents, I had to figure out another plan.

My first year at the academy had been incredibly difficult. Several good friends of mine ended up on a plane headed home because they couldn't be reformed. That wasn't my story. I had managed rather well. It turned out that the challenges I faced at Florida Air Academy were exactly what I needed. I had finally adapted to my surroundings. I learned to excel at my first real management position, despite being forced to endure the required social networking. During the course of the year, I even enlisted in an elite group of cadets who managed special groups that performed community service throughout Melbourne, Florida. In time, I was even awarded extra rank for my "exemplary behavior." But the moment I was just starting to get comfortable in my cocoon, I was forced to evolve yet again. God had other plans for me.

I didn't want to give up, move back to Michigan, and lose Rachel, but I couldn't continue to afford the tuition at Florida Air Academy without my parents backing. I searched as hard as I could for a way to continue my enrollment with Florida Air Academy, but as the months ebbed on, I ran into one roadblock after another. Every solution I proposed resulted in another rejection. I found out that as a 17-year-old minor without a car or job it was impossible to find an apartment to rent. I lost all hope, and I was forced to accept my fate.

At almost the same time that this door was shut, a Good Samaritan opened a window. Over the course of the past year, Rachel and I had grown close. Her family was my extended family. Rachel's grandma Margaret offered to take me in if I agreed to pay rent. She would rather know that I was safe in her house than in some low rent apartment complex. So I ended up moving in with Rachel, Margaret, Patricia, and Alex in a small ranch house.

Many years later, after I was released from yet another institution (this time it was the hospital), it was Margaret, Patricia, and Alex who drove up from Florida to help me recover. It needs to be said that along with all my trials and tribulations I have always been blessed with good friends and family to help me along the way. That is a fact that cannot be forgotten or overstated. Regardless of whether or not they understood what I was going through, they were always there to help where they could.

Now that I was free of my captivity at the air academy, I actually got to experience a little bit of what I had previously only dreamed of. Cape Canaveral and the Kennedy Space Center (KSC) was only about an hour north of where I was living, and now I was able to see the outside world. I watched several shuttle launches from on the beach. Watching a night launch was like watching the sun rise. It was amazing. Living on the Space Coast of Florida influenced my hopes and dreams. During the 1980s, the whole Space Coast was a thriving Mecca of industry that was built up around the technological vacuum that was the Kennedy Space Center. I didn't know how I would do it, but I wanted to work there some day. With KSC being only an hour away, engineers and those working on supplying products for the space industry made Melbourne their home. It's where they sent their children to school. I was going to go to school with the children of rocket scientists! I thought I had died and gone to Heaven!

When I registered to take classes at the public school in Melbourne, I was taking all college preparatory courses. This was the first time I had been introduced to college prep (or AP) courses in high school. I was elated. I got to take electronics and aeronautical engineering as high school classes. It was incredible! When I say aeronautical engineering, I mean there was a plane in the classroom that the students were helping to build. That was the coolest thing I had ever seen. So that fall I started going to my dream high school.

Socially, I was really getting along well too. Finally, I didn't feel like I was out of place, and I had friends. The classes were hard, but the instructors made learning fun for all of us. The class that I was having the most fun in was the aeronautical engineering class, and it was also my most difficult. A retired engineer taught the class. He had a dry sense of humor with a hippy-geek style to his attitude. He inspired me.

There was one project that I have to describe, because that was the turning point for me when I knew that I wanted to go into engineering. Growing up, my dad was an electronics technician for the railroad. My mother worked in printing and graphic design. I used to go out to see them at work. Both careers looked like they might be fun, but I didn't know that much about their daily routine. I had been putting together electronic kits with my dad from an early age, but I never really understood what engineering was while I was growing up. When I heard people talk about engineers, I thought they were talking about the guys that drove the train. I didn't know what the big deal about being an engineer was.

That first semester I finally realized that engineers were more than just the guys that drove the train. For me, the aeronautical engineering class was what dreams were made of. A partially constructed plane sat parked in the middle of the classroom. Going into that class, it was my understanding that the other students and I would be able to deconstruct a plane with drawings, plans, hardware tools, and basically learn about the systems the plane ran on.

Our first assignment was building a balsa wood plane. The professor told us that the lightweight balsa construction would teach us the importance of balance, thrust against velocity, and weight against gravity. At first, frustration hit me, because what I knew a balsa wood plane to be was one of those planes they sold at Walmart in the toy aisle for about a dollar. The balsa planes that I knew came all together in one little strip of balsa wood that had to be broken apart into its components. With these balsa wood planes, children had to fuss over them for about 20 minutes just to get the wing to go through the center slot. Then to add weight, the craftsmen always had to tape a dime to the end so that the plane would fly right. But it seemed to me that this was the extent of the engineering involved. So my first thought was why the heck did the professor want me to build one of those?

I didn't realize that real balsa wood planes are packaged in a kit that looks very much like a plastic model airplane kit. But instead of having a bunch of plastic parts that you break out of the molded pieces and snap together, it was altogether different. With a balsa wood kit, you get a number of sheets of balsa wood with some plans to tell you what you need to cut out to build it. You also get a propeller, a rubber band, and several sheets of tissue paper.

If you have ever seen a picture of a plane without the skin on it, then might have some understanding of the complexity. Each of those individual ribs and spars that make up the internal structure of the plane had to be individually cut out from the solid piece of balsa wood.

Of course, this required much more than just breaking the pre-cut pieces apart. It also took more to balance the plane than just taping a dime to the nose. I had to buy some additional supplies like a utility knife, some sand paper, and a jar of this paint type substance called dope.

To make a real balsa wood plane, you tediously cut out each individual rib of the plane with your utility knife. Next, as the builder, you need to construct the whole airplane from these little strips of balsa wood. If you are lucky, your balsa wood has the template drawn across the material. I wasn't so lucky. I had to learn how to cut out the template for each little piece from a large piece of paper. Then I had to individually tape these templates to the balsa wood and draw up my pattern before cutting it out. The patterns a young engineer works with are like the patterns tailors use to make dresses and clothes with.

After spending about 60 hours on my little masterpiece, I was finally able to put the tissue paper around its articulate little frame. Then I added the paint-like liquid called dope to the model. The dope served a couple of different purposes. First, I had to brush it on the frame like it was some sort of paint. This meant meticulously coating each individual spar of the model. This glues the tissue paper to the wood. Then I needed to apply the tissue paper to the frame as tightly as I could. Lastly, I needed to coat the tissue paper with the dope. To me it seemed kind of odd to paint the spars and to put the paper on it to hold it in place, and then, when the paper was on,

I had to paint it again to coat the whole surface. When the wet chemicals finally dried, the dope became tight. What was previously only a flimsy piece of tissue paper looked and felt like a paper-thin sheet of plastic. When I was eventually able to put on the little plastic nose cone on my work of art, I was so proud! I could not believe I had made an airplane out of those sheets of balsa wood, tissue paper, a rubber band, and that dope. To me, as a young teen, engineering was magical. I was sure that this was how children become inspired to create.

I got done with that project just in time. I just barely finished the plane over the weekend, and I was supposed to bring it into school the following Monday. I even went so far as to find a little shoebox to put it in so that I would be sure not to get it wet or somehow messed up on my way into school.

There I was coddling my precious creation in its custom-made shoebox hanger as I walked into my class just beaming with pride. As soon as class started, the teacher told us all to grab our planes so and to go out to the field to test them with him watching. Once we got outside, he instructed us to fly our planes. I was totally shocked. These planes were meant to fly? I had thought they were aesthetic. I assumed the teacher would only admire the beauty of our hard work.

I had grown up making the plastic models that either snap or are glued together. I learned quickly that those type of models break apart tragically if you manage to drop them or even look at them wrong. But I should have known that *these* planes were meant to fly. Why else would they have us put a little propeller on the nose with a rubber band? But even so, when the time came, very few of us students figured we would fly our creations on a windy field behind the school. Of course, "windy" is a relative term that increases exponentially based on how much time you spent putting together the model.

Either way, the teacher led his troops out to the

airfield. The time arrived for me to test my plane out. The rubber band engine was wound up. I let the frame sit on my hand, and then let go of the propeller. My plane took off beautifully. I really wish I could have taken a picture. My dive bomber flew up about 15 to 20 feet, before betraying me. It took a nose dive. The poor pilot who I imagined was flying my creation hit the ground with a smack. The frame didn't quite go Titanic on me, but the ship might just as well have sunk. My beautiful nose cone was crushed. I had a couple of small rips on the wings, but at least the wings stayed attached.

That was my first lesson in engineering. Thomas Edison was the first to admit his failures by insisting, "I have not failed. I have just found 10,000 way that won't work." After working my butt off that whole first semester, I managed to barely pass with just a "C". This was the lowest grade I got that semester. But the grade was a solid C. Better yet, my brain was hooked on engineering.

Seeing all that hard work subsequently break apart and just manage to net me a "C" was a *hard* lesson in engineering, but an exercise in failure is one that every engineer must absorb at some point. Albert Einstein realized that his first equation was wrong. He had to correct mistakes in his theory before pushing for his hypothesis to be published. Madame Curie earned a 1903 Nobel Prize in physics as well as chemistry in 1911, but before her awards came, she was denied acceptance to the University of Krakow because she was a woman. Therefore, Curie returned to Paris, where she had to learn to study in French only to pioneer the 1898 discovery of radium and polonium.

The lesson from the balsa wood airplane was that if you are ever going to design something, you need to start with a plan. Then that plan must meet some requirements. Those requirements need to achieve a goal that is the purpose of the design. In the case of my plane, the goal was that the plane needed to fly. The teacher wasn't showing us how to be elves that cut out toys from wood. Points were scored for how high the planes we built flew, how far our crafts flew, and how gracefully the models landed. A couple of pity points were given for style, but looks can't compensate for performance. There isn't a pilot in the world who thinks, "Boy, my plane is stylish," as he takes a nose dive into the hard earth. Essentially, the airplane I designed for class needed to work. Mine did work, but just marginally. But from that failure came success. From that point on, the professor gave me dreams. After experiencing the plethora of emotions that came with putting everything I have into creating something, I wanted to produce real designs. I wanted to design real systems that would function correctly and collect real data and meet real needs.

This partial success gave rise to further successes. I was finally challenged and had an interest to help drive me. I did much better in all my other classes during my time at the high school on the Space Coast. But more importantly, I now had a solid goal to work toward. I ended up with a 3.6 grade point average that semester, which was considered a B+ in my overall grades. So, I applied for an aeronautical engineering degree at Embry-Riddle Aeronautical University in Daytona Beach Florida. Thomas Edison would add up the challenges at the end of a project and say, "Many of life's failures are people who did not realize how close they were to success when they gave up."

Up to this point, my life was starting to turn around for the better. I was finally starting to realize those dreams that had seemed so distant when I was growing up in Michigan. I had a happy life with Rachel and her family. Now I also aspired for a future career in engineering. Both were in Florida. Yet Florida turned out to be major failure. Embry-Riddle denied my acceptance. The news devastated me.

Not long after, Rachel left me. We broke up in October and I was forced to continue living with her and her family until the semester was done in December. My emotions were shaken. The one-two punch mortified me. The combination came quickly within days of each other. Rachel's letter said, "I know that we have been dating for over a year. Even though we're both living under the same roof, can we just be friends?" Just when I felt like I was starting to see the light at the end of the long tunnel, it turned out to be a train. I was disillusioned by life in general.

I had to refocus. My first goal was to get into Embry-Riddle so that I could study engineering. Once again, I was forced to use my problem-solving skills to find a way of working within the system. The institution didn't accept my studies in Aeronautical Engineering. I thought about it and tried to break it down into smaller, more manageable steps. Aeronautics is the science surrounding flight. But outside of my aeronautical engineering class in high school, I had never had any aeronautical training. Although I really enjoyed the class, a "C" wasn't going to get me anywhere.

So I thought about what I did have experience in. In my electronics class, I had managed a solid "A". I had also spent many hours working on electronics projects with my dad while I was growing up. How do I link these skills in electronics with my desire to pursue aviation (and eventually space)? What I found out in my aeronautical engineering class was that avionics are the electronic instruments that are used for aviation. Avionics itself is derived from the combination of aviation and electronics. I figured that I really liked electronics so what could it hurt? I figured that the tinkering I had done in electronics with my dad would also help me with my new career pursuit. Because I didn't give up, my re-application for a degree in avionics engineering was accepted.

CHAPTER 4

Psalm 23:4 – Even though I walk through the darkest valley, I will fear no evil, for you are with me; your rod and your staff, they comfort me.

Being accepted into Embry Riddle gave me a new plan and a new goal in life. But without Rachel wanting to continue our relationship, I returned to Michigan deflated. Being rejected in October was bad enough, but I still lived under the same roof with Rachel for two months. It was almost like rubbing salt on an open wound. Once the fall semester finished, I traded the warm Florida winters for the snow-covered landscape of my parents' house in Grand Rapids, Michigan. By January, I was back at Hudsonville High School and shoveling snow to get from my parents' front door to the driveway.

Spring came. The winter thawed. And in April, I woke up disoriented and barely alive in a hospital after being hit by a truck. In a brief instant in time, my new goal in life was reduced to staying alive and re-learning how to walk.

I was in intensive care for four days, but I only remember the point where I "came to" at some point toward the end of that time. I have been told by others that I was drifting in and out of consciousness the whole time. For me, there was a definite epoch in time when I fully remember regaining a foothold on reality.

Waking up that first night after the accident reminded me of a night I had spent in the hospital as a child. I was diagnosed with asthma at a very young age, so I was no stranger to the hospital. There were several times for me as a kid when I would get hit with an asthma attack and be rushed to the emergency room. I remember getting a shot of something to ease my breathing. After that shot, there was a time where my lungs loosened up and I could breathe again. Then it was time to go home.

Most of my hospital exposure was just that, a quick visit. There was that one time, about seven, when I stayed overnight because they had taken my tonsils out, but that was it. For a kid of seven, being in the hospital had kind of a fun feel to it. It was exciting to stay away from home. I remember pushing the nurse's button, and they would bring me treats. After my tonsils were taken out in surgery that day, I made good use of this button, and as a result, I had an endless supply of ice-cream.

But then came nighttime. After the visiting hours had ended and the anesthesia had worn off, pain woke me. It was the middle of the night, and it was very dark, but not totally dark. There was a cold blue fluorescent light coming from somewhere out in the hall, and I remember hearing the echo of clicking shoes on the tile somewhere. It was also physically cold. It wasn't cold to the point where frost could form, but it was an uncomfortable cold nonetheless. In my semi-conscious state, I had no idea where I was.

As the pain forced my seven-year-old body awake, I could feel the cold gnawing at me. Then when I came into consciousness, the antiseptic smell assaulted my senses. It was foreign and cold, and I was in pain. In my confused state, I forgot about the magic nurse's button. After what seemed like hours, I managed to moan loud enough for one of the nurses to hear me. They came in and covered my one thin sheet with a thin scratchy blanket. A couple of scratchy blankets more eventually eased the cold. The pain remained, and that night I was never comfortable.

This was the same state of confused pain I remember waking to at the hospital after my accident. I discovered a similar scratchy blanket along with the same cold and overpowering antiseptic smells from years before. It wasn't too long before I figured out where I must be, although I had no memory of how I might have gotten there. This time, instead of a throbbing pain in my throat from the tonsil surgery, a searing pain in my leg had drawn me out of my semi-comatose state. Eventually, in one of my more lucid states, I realized I had lost about four days of my life between the date of my accident and the date I started to remember my time in the hospital. You could say I lost my memory of those first four days. But losing something indicates that you want it back. I don't want those memories back.

Also, unlike when I had my tonsils out, the wounds ran too deep. There was no amount of ice-cream that was going to satisfy my needs. What's more, the pain medication barely managed the pain. Pain was my new companion, and when I was awake, it was a constant battle to keep it from overpowering me. I don't really know how long this lasted. Eventually, that pain subsided. But in one instant in time, my life changed course drastically.

I really should (and do) consider myself lucky. During my stay at Butterworth, I went through many subsequent operations. I had many hours of operation to repair my leg. They put in a surgical steel rod and numerous pins. I also had two vertebrae sewn together in my neck. The surgery on my neck was critical, because there was a real danger that I would move my neck wrong and sever my spinal cord. As it was, it was a miracle that my spinal cord wasn't severed during the accident. I had bone fragments removed from my pelvis where my pelvis was fractured in two places. I had plastic surgery on the left side of my face. I was told that someday I could come back and they would remove the scar on the left side of my face.

Many years later, I did have an operation. I had the steel bar removed from my leg. But I never went back to fix the scars on my face, and I never will. That scar isn't big. But along with that steel rod and those pins, I keep that scar as a reminder of where I have come from and how far I have yet to go. We all need things to remind us of who we are. As of this writing, I have that steel rod and those pins in a drawer somewhere. Someday, I might lose them. But I will never lose that scar. That scar and I have been through a lot together.

There were many procedures needed to fix my broken body. After each procedure, it seemed that my prognosis was slightly better. Although each statement fell just slightly short of reassuring. There were many hours of operations. And there would be many years to heal. My healing had just begun.

Because of all the hard work that was done by all those doctors those first couple of weeks, I was eventually told I might be able to walk without a cane. The doctors also assured me that, with a lot of rehabilitation and therapy, I would be able to live my life almost as good as before the accident. But there was never anyone who could expand on that statement. I remember vividly thinking to myself, *Almost as good? Where is the hope in that?* To me, this would be equivalent to a football coach telling his team, "You know, team, if we all work really hard together, we might not lose as badly as we did last time! If we really work hard, we might even tie!" That doesn't make any sense. When you encourage someone, they should have something to aim for. But at the time, that wasn't the type of hope and encouragement I was given.

Those first two weeks in Butterworth went by pretty quickly for me. I guess it probably helped that I had spent the first four days or so semi-comatose in intensive care and most of the rest of the time sleeping. But there was one point, during one of my more lucid moments, when I remembered that I hadn't studied for a test that was coming up in one of my classes.

At this point, I was out of the intensive care unit and was on the road to recovery, but I was still in very bad shape. As it happened, the test was during one of those four days that I couldn't remember. But my initial panic was intensified by the fact that I had no idea what the date was. I remember thinking about how important it was that I get back home so that I could study for that test. I realized later that I had long missed the test and expected to take it due to my circumstances. I was so grateful to learn this fact that I still remember the feeling to this day. I don't remember which subject it was, but I remember that I had gotten out of that test.

When I look back on it now, it seems funny that amidst all the tragedy there was still a feeling of relief that I didn't have to take that test. I often wonder why we get so caught up on these menial problems. It seems so ridiculous when we look at it from outside of our normal perspectives. I still have times when I wonder if we have it all wrong. Why does the human race seem to get all caught up in things that mean so little in the grand scheme of things?

When I attended Embry-Riddle much later, a wise sage professor from Columbia taught me about a concept that applies directly to this. He taught me that in Columbia (and I am sure many other places) they have a different concept of time. They actually had a couple of different "measurements of time." Not by the watch of course, but in the way that they looked at their life.

There is the normal time you experience most every day as you live your life and perform your normal routines. But then there is also "special time." These special times are the times you need to set aside and force yourself to keep special. Special times are those that you always want to hold onto. These aren't necessarily scheduled and usually occur in a spontaneous fashion. But these times should not be registered using any normal clock.

An example might be your first kiss. Another would be the time you hit the ball out of the park and you could hear the cheer of the crowd as you ran around the bases and back into home. For me, a special moment I cling to is when each of my sons fell asleep on my lap. Sometimes, on a rare occasion, I had both on my lap sleeping at the same time when one was a toddler and one was a newborn. Even though my legs fell asleep, I didn't want to wake them. These memories came many years after my accident, but I remember them like it was yesterday. They are my special times—the day I stopped time. Yes, it is true. All things must come to an end. But in our minds, there is always room for more of this special time. These are the times you want to hold onto when you are just getting by. I wish with all my heart that I could somehow give those memories to my younger self just so I could have had that thread of hope to hold on to as I was going through that bad time in my life.

There are many other examples of these special times over the years, and I hope and pray there are many more. It is funny how something like getting knocked on the side of the head can change one's perspective. In many ways, I hope no one reading this will ever have to go through something like my accident. But if you do, it is important to keep in mind that all things come to an end. Even the bad things.

In total, my time at Butterworth Hospital lasted about two weeks. Four days of that time was spent in intensive care.

The following is an excerpt from hospital consultation records that are dated April 14, 1989:

Mr. Meek is an 18 year old, left handed, high school student who was found in a pickup truck in the front seat unresponsive to verbal stimuli. There had been a collision where another vehicle struck the pickup truck broadside on the driver's door side. Enroute with the emergency crew his Glasgow coma score was 10. On arrival at Butterworth Hospital his Glasgow coma score was 14 to 15.

This man's speech does not betray any gross dyphasia nor dysarthria. Simple naming was accurate for familiar objects. His orientation was clear that he was in an accident and that he is now in Butterworth Hospital in Grand Rapids and he was able to tell me that his face required some repair and that he injured his neck and that required fusion. Initially he tended to forget that he had an injury of the left lower extremity but then recalled that that was broke. He did not indicate he felt there was any head injury, though that was alluded to in the chart. He knew that it was Friday and that he had been in the hospital about a week and a half, his injury being on 4-4. He was off on one calendar date on the date currently. He described his surgery as being on "Tuesday" when in fact it was on the previous Thursday, about eight days ago. When asked about current events he could not relate much of anything he had heard on TV or radio. When given seven digits he could repeat them easily forward and could reverse four. New information in the form of a man's name, address, make and color of a car, however, were not retained at a normal level after 15 to 20 minutes delay, even though we drilled the information several times and he was asked to be sure to try to recall it.

On an outline of the map of Michigan, he was able to accurately place Detroit and Mackinaw, but was less clear on Lansing and Grand Rapids. On an outline of the map of Florida, he persistently said that his high school academy, which he states is in Melbourne, was on the east coast, however, he placed the dot right near Tampa on the west coast. I attempted to point out the error to him once or twice but he did not comprehend it. On a blank circle he was asked to put numerals around it as if it were a clock face. He got most of them in the correct sequence but there were spacing errors and bunching of numerals together indicating possible perception difficulties.

Another report dated April 29, 1989 gives more insight into the extent of my head injury:

Memory functions were further assessed with the CVLT,

which is a task requiring the learning of a 16-item grocery list over successive trials. Mr. Meek was able to recall 13 items after five trials, and 11 items, after a 20-minute delay with interpolated activity. The latter is definitely an impaired score. This stands somewhat in contrast with his average recall of stories on the WMS-R, as documented in the 4-26 Psychology Initial Evaluation note. This suggests that Mr. Meek can recall verbally information when it is represented in a meaningful context, but that he has difficulty recalling more factual, discrete, or unrelated information. Several problem-solving tasks were administrated. Mr. Meek obtained unimpaired scores on tests requiring the modification of matching or sorting strategies on the basis of principals that were not specified a priori after each matching or sorting attempt (BCT, WCST). He also was able to engage in problem solving with tangible materials as evidenced by his average time to complete three trials on a task where he had to place blocks of various sizes and shapes into their corresponding spaces on a form board while blindfolded (TPT). At the same time, it should be noted that he did not improve very much with practice on the TPT, suggesting relatively reduced efficiency of learning. He also had no idea of the correct location of test materials on the board when he was asked (without prior warning) to draw the board from memory after the task was completed. All of these findings suggest that Mr. Meek can engage in novel problem-solving. He can definitely profit from feedback and learn from his mistakes. However, his learning is not as efficient as it probably was premorbidly and he may need more extended time and more practice with tasks than usual. Also, he does not spontaneously or incidentally pick up information as he goes along with tasks as he probably did before.

I include these un-edited excerpts as insight to my situation. I am not a doctor and can certainly not give you an accurate translation. But I am pretty sure it is stating, quite accurately, that I was messed up. Other excerpts effectively state that the doctors were not sure how well I would do in a scholastic environment because they weren't sure I would ever be able to communicate as effectively as I was able to prior to the accident. Well, I will let my readers be the judge of that one.

My situation wasn't all that spectacular medically. But it serves as an example of the type of analysis that our medical examiners can perform. What they can't perform is an analysis of what is inside—such as the motivations, hopes and dreams that keep us going. This isn't scientifically measurable, but it must be considered. The doctors who examined me had no idea what drove or motivated me, so this important element was always missing from any of their reports.

I hadn't seen these records prior to my requesting them in 2012. Not that I am at all surprised by the extent of the injuries I had sustained, but in many ways, I feel fortunate that I had not seen the reports earlier. When you are forcing yourself to get out of bed in the morning and take yet another step (sometimes literally as well as figuratively), it is all you can do to keep on going.

Sometimes, that is all you can do and all you need to do. You need to just keep on going, even if there is no end in sight. It's like riding a bike up a long steep hill. As long as you press forward, you have to endure the pain. You are sometimes forced to slow down and maybe even walk your bike, but I have always found that it is better to keep moving even if it's at a slower pace. When you stop, your muscles tighten up, and it makes it much harder to start back up again. That was what I had to do those first few years. I had to keep going, because I knew that, as soon as I stopped, my muscles would tighten up, and I would find it that much harder to start back up again. So, I kept myself going to school. I kept pushing forward a day at a time. On some days, I had to keep myself putting one foot in front of the other—both literally and figuratively.

While you are going up, it can seem unbearable at

times. But when you reach the top and look back at how far you have come, it can be exhilarating and frightening at the same time, particularly as you look back at what you went through. That is where I am at now.

CHAPTER 5

Colossians 2:8 — See to it that no one takes you captive through hollow and deceptive philosophy, which depends on human tradition and the elemental spiritual forces of this world rather than on Christ.

My two weeks at Butterworth hospital were just the beginning. I got a new room with a view at Mary Free Bed Rehabilitation Center in Grand Rapids, Michigan. Initially, it seemed to me that I had moved from one room of antiseptic smells and scratchy blankets to another. The only difference was location.

I learned, however, the big difference was in the type of treatment and analysis I was receiving. At Butterworth Hospital, the primary focus of the doctors was to stabilize my condition and treat the physical ailments. This did include some analysis of my cognition and different aspects of my head injury, but this wasn't the primary focus of their efforts. The success criteria for Butterworth Hospital, apparently, was to ensure that I was physically functional to the extent that was possible to justify leaving the hospital.

At Mary Free Bed, the focus was on rehabilitation. The doctors there assessed my situation and taught me how to adapt to life after my accident. This meant that, along with learning about the effects of a head injury, I was also working to overcome the physical limitations I had. I was taught how to walk on crutches and eventually relearned how to walk. Then therapists assessed my cognitive skills, such as how to find my way out of a department store and back to the car.

During this time, I underwent a series of different tests by doctors of several different disciplines. These included physical therapy, occupational therapy, recreational therapy, and psychology to better define my treatment and recovery plan. So, to greatly simplify the 6 plus months of therapy I went through, physical therapy worked to strengthen my abilities, such as walking with crutches, and to test, evaluate, and expand my physical capabilities, such as range of motion of my leg. In addition, an occupational therapist worked with me to expand my abilities with regards to occupational skills, such as cooking, cleaning, sorting, and so forth. Recreational therapy was always my favorite. Some of the best sessions involved remote control cars, board games, and swimming. I am not sure what is therapeutic about board games, but at least it helped me to keep my mind off my current situation and it helped with the overarching sense of loneliness and boredom.

By the time I got to Mary Free Bed Rehabilitation Center, I was starting to become a little more aware of my surroundings, and I got a chance to piece together a little bit more of what had happened to me. Since I don't remember anything just prior to leaving my parents' house until four days later, I must rely on what others have told me happened during that time. The last thing I remembered prior to waking up in the hospital was being at my parent's house and that I needed to go to work at the theater in Holland, Michigan. I found out from my dad that when I first hopped into my car that night, my car didn't start, and so he had let me borrow his truck. Prior to that night, my car had been pretty dependable; there wasn't any reason why it shouldn't have started. Yet it chose that night to give me some difficulty. Of course, after the accident when I tried it months later, it gave me no problems with starting at all.

It was about sunset when I drove up to the 2-way stop sign that was about a quarter mile from our house and stopped. I pulled into the intersection, and just then, a truck came over the hill to my left and slammed into my driver's side door. I don't remember even getting into the truck. I don't remember anything until four days later. But, once again, I don't really want to.

Even so, based on the information I have pieced together, there are a number of peculiarities that I would like to point out. The events leading up to the accident have gone through my head countless times.

First off, prior to that night, my car was fairly dependable. There should have been no reason why it wouldn't start like it had so many times before. If it had started on the first attempt, then there probably wouldn't have been any accident. Then again, if I did eventually get my car started and enough time had passed whereas to put me in the path of that same truck, but this time in my little car, things would have ended up quite different.

My car was a small four-door station wagon and there is no way I would have made it out alive. As it was, my dad's full-sized pickup truck was in three distinct pieces 100 feet or so from the point of impact.

In one scenario, there is no accident at all. While in the other scenario, I end up dead. Not surprising, as I am sure is the case for many other accident survivors, I was left to wonder why God led me to this fate. In an instant, it seemed like my whole life had been destroyed, yet I was destined to continue to live it.

On the way to the hospital, my heart stopped. I don't have any details of this. I do remember having a heaven-sent dream where I had an overwhelming feeling of peace. It was not like a normal dream, but different somehow, more vivid, but at the same time more calming. If that doesn't make any sense, then I apologize. But it isn't the type of thing that is easy to describe. I don't remember exactly when I had this dream. I do know that it was some time very shortly after the accident.

To better describe the dream, imagine that your body is

very small and you are floating on a leaf on a smooth pond driven by a gentle current. Then someone drops a pebble into the pond, but you don't see the pebble fall and you don't see where it landed. You only see large ripples coming at you along the surface of the water. These ripples force you to hang on to your leaf for fear of falling off. As time progresses, the ripples grow smaller. But because you didn't see the pebble go in, you don't know where the ripples originated. All you know is that the ripples are pushing your leaf in an opposite direction from their origination point.

The ripples finally become barely perceivable, and eventually, it is over and you are back adrift. Once it is over, you only know that it happened. You have a memory of the ripples happening, but now it is just a memory. The ripples are gone. The pond is peaceful again. But now your leaf is headed in a slightly different direction.

I now realize that this dream was a reflection of my future life. In one instant, my direction was changed. I have no memory of what caused the ripples in my pond, but in that one instant, my life changed, and I was going to take an altogether different path than I had planned. In the dream, I was an observer. I could see the peaceful tranquility of the ripples and how they effected the stillness of the water. But it was okay. That was supposed to happen. I could see the ripples growing smaller and smaller to the point where eventually they would become imperceptible. Yet I knew that it was all the intent of the one who had dropped the stone.

After my time as an inpatient at Mary Free Bed, they let me go home with the understanding that I was to go through outpatient therapy for the next 4-6 months at the Mary Free Bed Outpatient Center. My new schedule began each day with going to high school for a couple of hours, but then someone picked me up at noon to take me over to Mary Free Bed Outpatient Center for the afternoon. This was to continue through my graduation in May, and then I was to go to Mary Free Bed full time after graduation. I was assured that I was to be given my diploma at the end of summer, assuming I continued my studies part time in addition to being tutored while at Mary Free Bed.

During my time at the outpatient center, I went through many different tests. I was still sleeping quite a bit. But I was getting a bit better and only needed to sleep a couple of hours during the afternoon rather than for most of it. I went through more physical therapy, occupational therapy, psychological testing and therapy, and recreational therapy. Along with my therapy, I was also assigned a special tutor at Mary Free Bed to help tutor me in English literature.

It was during one of my psychological therapy sessions where I ran into my first point of contention. Part of the therapy was to get a better understanding of head injuries so that I would better understand what to expect. I was told that after the age of 12 (I was then 18), the brain stopped growing. That meant that, no matter what I did, I would never get back the full capability I had before the accident. Although the neurons would remap themselves to work around the damaged sections of the brain, I would never again have that full functionality. Along with this, I was told to accept the fact that maybe engineering wasn't in my cards.

No way! I was not and am still not a doctor. But this flawed version of reality was not something I intended to accept. There was a reason God pulled me through that accident in one piece. Everything in my heart told me they were wrong and that I was right, and I wasn't about to give up on my dreams. This was one of my key decision points.

At this point I need to tell you a little bit more about my childhood. Like I said before, I had asthma growing up. I was diagnosed with asthma when I was about 4 years old. This was long before asthma was a household name, and at that point, many of today's treatments weren't around. I still remember lying on the couch wheezing while my mom and grandma hovered over me with a homeopathic remedy called a mustard plaster. It was like a hot towel that had a combination of playdough and spicy brown mustard caked on it. They hoped that if you placed this steamy concoction on the victim's chest, then the vapors made the bad asthma demons go away. In reality, it burned like fire and caused you to forget about breathing long enough to get the cursed thing off your chest. This was cure number one.

The doctor's cure at the time wasn't a whole lot better. They gave me a cylinder of some kind, like today's version of an inhaler. The cylinder had a little fan inside that would spin as you compressed the cylinder. Then the cure came in the form of a little capsule that looked like it was filled with a million small beads. You put the capsule in the cylinder, and then when you compressed the thing, the capsule was crushed open and the little fan blew all those little beads into your lungs. After a fit of coughing, presto, you're cured of your asthma! Except I wasn't.

Now, given such a background, I did not put a whole lot of faith in doctors' opinions. I was sure they had the best of intentions, but I was also sure they were dead wrong, and I was determined not to let it stop me. There is a reason why the doctors call their work a "practice." They had saved my life; that is an absolute fact I cannot dispute and will not deny. But we are all just human.

Science, as it relates to the brain and the body, is not yet an exact science. There are many variables that we, as a human race, just don't collectively understand. So, I was not about to give up all hope of a future as an engineer. I was sure I needed to keep fighting. I knew that God had pulled me through such an awful, impossible situation for a reason. So I made the decision to press on. I wasn't sure where this path would lead, but I needed to follow it and just trust that it would work. I made the decision to continue my plans to go to school for engineering.

City, New York.

Well, the analogy I would give for my accident isn't quite as drastic, but I will give it to you anyway. Imagine driving a car and chucking a golf ball out the window. My survival would be much like the golf ball bouncing down the road through a cornfield to end up getting a hole in one at some golf course 6 miles away. That would be my analogy. There were just too many different things that could have gone wrong, but somehow didn't.

CHAPTER 6

Proverbs 4:25 – Let your eyes look straight ahead; fix your gaze directly before you.

Concentration was a real challenge to learning after my head injury. My brain skipped frames, like randomly missing frames from an old movie. In some cases, it would be like someone randomly changing the channel while you were totally immersed in a TV show, only to happen again once you've started getting into the new story. Dealing with this reality was very discouraging. It was easy to lose all hope. Sometimes, it wasn't as discouraging as it was enraging.

Imagine being well into your favorite TV show and someone comes along and gets right in your face and starts picking his nose while asking absurd questions. Then the dog starts whining at the door wanting to go out, and the cat jumps on the table and starts drinking your milk. Then you suddenly remember you are trying to watch TV. Come to think of it, you don't have a dog. So, where did the dog come from? Boy, is that ever confusing. But what about the cat? Wait. You don't have a cat either. What's going on? Wait, what TV show is this? "My Little Pony?" But you were watching "Malcolm in the Middle!" You suddenly want to scream. Only then, you realize you are in a movie theater. Wait. You're on a horse. Argh. It's just too much. You need to sleep. Welcome to my head injury.

Yes, looking back on it, I want to laugh. It is all so funny. But it was honestly that confusing at times. I just wanted to wake up and be completely healed, but it took time and a lot of sleep. Along with it, I quickly learned that loud noises and lots of distractions were not good for me.

So now you have a glimpse of my life as I was trying to get it started again. After a while, I realized I wasn't in control, but there were patterns. When things started to get confusing, I needed to sleep. When I started to get angry, I needed some quiet. Sometimes, quiet was all I needed. Yet knowing about the patterns and allowing for these necessities are two different things.

Going to Embry-Riddle that first fall meant everything to me. The doctors tried to convince me to abandon my dreams by telling me I wasn't mentally capable of college, that because of the severity of my brain injuries, I would never make it. Their words became a form of reverse psychology; I had to prove them wrong. No one was going to tell me what I couldn't do.

Going off to college in August, just 4 months after the accident, meant I had beaten back the naysayers and continued down the path I had planned for my life. But the first fall semester came too quickly for me, and I had to admit, I still needed time to heal. I felt betrayed by my own body. I was depressed, disillusioned, and worse yet, I started to lose hope.

That first summer and into the first year, I eventually figured out the most important rule for my post-traumatic lifestyle: be gentle with yourself. I learned there was really nothing I could do to hurry up this healing process. Every time I tried to ignore my needs, I wore myself out. I got depressed. I got angry. It was all too easy to lose hope. Yet somewhere in the back of my mind was the other statement by the doctors: "With a lot of hard work, you could live almost as well as you had before the accident." That statement and many others had the effect of pushing me to continue. It was almost like an invisible coach that motivated me to take an extra step and to push just a little harder.

I wasn't ready to give up. Yet I had to accept that

things worked differently. I had to re-learn who I was. I was still the young man who wanted to go into engineering. I was still the young man who wanted to go to Embry-Riddle. My goals were the same, but how I was going to accomplish those goals had to change. I had to learn to be gentle with myself. I was forced to compromise. I needed extra sleep, and more importantly, I needed time.

I decided to start college in the fall, just as I had planned. Instead of starting at Embry-Riddle over a thousand miles from home, I decided to start by taking some of the basic English courses at the community college in Grand Rapids, Michigan. This was only 30 minutes or so from my parents' house, and it gave me the opportunity to try out college before submitting myself to fulltime coursework or invest too much money into it. This turned out to be the best solution anyway, because I found out later that not all classes transfer when you switch schools. But there wasn't any problem transferring those first year English courses.

After all I had been through to that point, it was surprising that going to college wasn't all that difficult for me. This is in part due to the fact I only took 1 class at a time: English 101 in the fall and English 102 in the spring. In truth, these classes were easy enough for me since I had been taking English all summer at Mary Free Bed with a private tutor. By the time I got to take my first class at Grand Rapids Community College, I already had several months of Shakespeare under my belt. So, I was surprised to learn that the first assignment was to read and do a report on Macbeth, which is a book that I had spent the summer working on. Needless to say, I ended up doing very well in that first English class and the second English class was pretty easy for me as well.

After two successful college courses under my belt and over a year of healing, I made arrangements to begin school the following August at Embry-Riddle Aeronautical

University in Daytona Beach, Florida.

CHAPTER 7

Romans 8:28 – And we know that in all things God works for the good of those who love him, who have been called according to his purpose.

Going to Embry-Riddle that following year was like nothing I had been through before. When I had gone to military school, I spent most of my energy either trying to work within the rules that were being imposed on me or finding ways to creatively avoid them. When I moved in with Rachel and her family, I could just focus on my schoolwork. Dinners were made for me. Life carried on as I always remembered it. When I came home after the accident, I focused on the couple of classes I was taking and trying to work within my means.

However, when I first started Embry-Riddle, no one was there to tell me what it was I needed to do. My parents were still paying off the loans they had incurred from my time at Florida Air Academy. They had done their part. It was time for me to make it on my own.

It was my decision to go to college, and therefore it was my responsibility to pay for it. I found out right away that this was a lot harder to do than I could have imagined. In spite of my success in the community college courses, I did not have good grades in high school and did not have any possibility of an academic scholarship, so I had to depend on the government's student loan program. I had chosen to go to an expensive private university, so I had to make sacrifices. To me, at the time, it seemed like the cheap route meant living off campus and buying my own food rather than living on campus and purchasing an expensive meal plan.

It seemed all too perfect at the time. I had a car, I had a little bit of money saved up for food, and I didn't want to live back in a military school type setting where everyone was crammed into one little room with four beds. I knew that I would have to have roommates, but I figured that it wouldn't be so bad as long as we had our own space. I also figured I would just get a job to help pay for the utilities, food, and books. That was the path I chose or at least the path I was forced to take.

I did end up getting a pretty nice little apartment. It was a great little apartment complex right on the river about four miles from campus, but it was also only about four miles from the beach—Daytona Beach that is. I was all set to begin my new life.

Once I had my apartment squared away, it was time for me to get registered for my classes at school. Like all the other incoming freshmen, I had to take my placement tests before I could register for my classes. These were the two four hour timed tests that you needed to take to determine the classes for each of the subjects you would be placed in. If you did well on these, then you can potentially skip the very first 100 level classes (such as math or English) and enroll in one of the higher level classes.

What made these tests really difficult for me was the head injury. What made these tests impossible for me was the fact that they were timed. As I have already said, time is irrelevant when you have a head injury, especially when you are sitting there, pencil in hand, taking your math test when someone changes the channel. "Oh look! There is Fido at the door again. Wait a second! What do you mean my time is up?!" I didn't have to take any English placement tests because, as I have said, I took my first two college English classes at Grand Rapids Community College. But I did miserably for my math placement test.

But bombing my math placement test was just the beginning for me. To make matters worse, I was not at all familiar with how things were done at a large university. After the placement tests were out of the way, each freshmen was ushered into a big hall that was set up for admissions. It was our job to show up at this hall during a scheduled 2-hour block of time on a day that was scheduled for freshman admissions. So, along with a few hundred of my fellow classmates, I showed up to meet with my assigned guidance counselor.

In that hall, at that specified time, there was a row of tables set up alphabetically for students to come in and talk to a counselor. If your last name started with "L-M," you were assigned whatever guidance counselor was standing at that table. It was loud. It was chaotic. I had a bad head injury and was completely new to this whole sort of process. That is why I didn't question the decision when my counselor looked at my math scores and placed me in the absolute lowest level of math.

This was the math class that they stuck people in that had absolutely no desire to do anything with math in their career field. But because he was my guidance counselor and he was the one in charge of assigning this sort of thing, I didn't question the decision. What I should have done was held up the line behind me and questioned, "As an engineering student, why am I being placed in the lowest level of basic math for aviators?" But I didn't do that. So, in limiting my semesters to 12 credits and adding several additional math classes, my degree was going to take me a long time to complete. But I knew in my heart that I was being led to pursue a career in engineering, so I kept going.

Those first couple of weeks were like a blur for me. Because I was part of the group of incoming freshmen, it also meant I was one of the last ones to choose my class schedule. So the basic math course I got stuck in was at 7:30 AM. I had a couple of other morning classes, but then I had a nice long stretch where I didn't have any classes. My last class started at 4:00 PM. Because I lived off campus, it meant I got to drive home after my last morning class sometime around 10:00 AM.

Going home was easy. There was a two-lane road running east and west that led straight from campus to my apartment. About two miles down that road, right between my apartment and the college, there was a fairly large road where a number of fraternities were headquartered.

I had never thought much about going to a fraternity. First off, I wasn't sure what it was all about. I didn't really understand why you would want to hang around in a big house with a bunch of guys. But one day within that first couple of weeks, I drove by one of those fraternities that had a big triangle and an X on it. While I was at a stop sign, a guy handed out fliers that said something along the lines of "Pledge Delta-Chi" on it. I asked him which one was "delta-chee." He looked at me a little funny, but at least smiled and then told me it was pronounced "delta k-eye." He told me that I should at least stop by, because they had a big beach volleyball court behind the house and they were desperate for more players.

At the time, I was just on my way back to the apartment for my first afternoon nap, but I figured I would at least go see what one of those houses looked like on the inside. I was pleasantly surprised when I got there. There was a big living room area with a number of couches and there were a number of guys sitting around watching some sort of science show. I thought how cool it was that they got to sit around and watch cool shows like that on a big screen TV. It didn't take me too long to feel welcome. Not long after, I decided to try it out for a semester and see what fraternity life was all about.

Going over to the Delta Chi house was a lot more interesting than I initially thought it would be. During the week, there were always a number of people just hanging out. Then on the weekends, there was always some sort of party. Often, they had some sort of theme to the party. I was never much of a party goer, but the parties there were somehow different and almost always included a number of games of beach volleyball. Mostly, I liked the big family atmosphere. There were always people around, going back and forth from school. If you have ever seen the TV show "Cheers" where all the bar patrons yell, "Norm!", when the big guy walks in the door, then you have an idea of what it was like. Also, very much like "Cheers," everyone in Delta Chi knew my name.

As a "pledge" or someone who is trying to become a full-fledged member of the fraternity, I was grouped with the other pledges. They were assigned to be my comrades as we were being initiated. Part of the process of going through as a pledge required that you learn different things about the history of the fraternity. This also meant you had to learn the Greek alphabet. Throwing us together as a group and getting us to work together was one of the absolute highlights of my time at Embry-Riddle. It was one of those bonding experiences that really brought us together as a group.

This bonding experience had a whole new meaning a month or so after I started pledging Delta Chi. It was then that my trusty car decided to die. Luckily, it chose to die just a block or two from the fraternity. So here I was, carless, a very new college freshman going to school a couple of thousand miles from home, had very little money to my name, was still reeling from the effects of my head injury, and had a need to travel four miles from campus in each direction a couple of times a day because of my class schedule. That was when I learned the phrase, "Cooperate to graduate." That meant we were all in it together. We were all working toward a common goal. We all had different strengths and weaknesses, but when you really need the help, it was your friends who were there to help you. When you see one of your friends struggling, it was up to you to step up to the plate.

Being a pledge had its challenges. But the whole purpose behind having us memorize the history, the Greek alphabet, and other seemingly meaningless facts was that the fraternity brothers were trying to force us to work together as a team. So, when my car died, all I had to do was ask my fraternity brothers for help. I immediately had over 30 guys caravanning down the road to help bring my car back to my apartment. Out of my 30 friends, one correctly identified that the problem with my car was the timing belt. I had no idea what a timing belt was. But lo and behold, it was worn out. Luckily it didn't cause any engine damage when it went out, or I would have had much bigger problems. The same guy even offered to help me fix the car. The only problem was that he needed to get his timing light from back at his parents' house, but he wasn't planning on going home until the end of the semester. So, I was stuck.

I needed to find a way to and from school. I had two roommates that both went to Embry-Riddle with me. So, the first thing I did was see if they could give me a ride on their way to or from school. As it turned out, one of my roommates worked for the school in the traffic enforcement department. He needed to go to school early to work. He helped me out immensely by giving me a ride to school every day. He also helped me get a job with the traffic enforcement department.

That worked really well for me, because I could walk around campus and work during that long stretch of time between my morning and afternoon classes. But I still needed to nap. This only got worse when I was forced to walk a lot more. Luckily, my fellow pledges were there to help. They offered me a place to hide away from the afternoon sun. So, when I reached the limit of how much I could work, I would return to their dorm room and take a nap on their couch. Although there were certainly hardships, I made it through that first semester with a little help from my friends.

You might be wondering what led me to believe that God was leading me on through that first semester. Well, believe it or not, there were several absolute miracles taking place under the surface. First off, I was forced by my limited funding to take that apartment off campus, but I learned many lessons and met many friends along the way. Even though I was forced into that choice, God was right there as my safety net.

It was God that led me to that fraternity. You might think that a fraternity is just another word for party house, but I am here to say that those frat boys were true friends. They always helped me out and tried to push me down the right path in school. Aside from that whole ordeal when they helped me out with my car, there were several times when they literally saved me or helped me out in one way or another.

I know there were times when I helped them out too, although the specifics elude me. I really learned that I needed to "cooperate to graduate." I felt like I had grown up as a loner, but I was no longer alone. Even people who didn't like me were right there to lend me some food or give me a ride.

The next safety net God threw me was my roommates. It was one of my roommates who helped me to get the job with the traffic enforcement department. That wasn't even close to one of my favorite part time jobs, but it allowed me the flexibility I needed to work and nap between classes. Because I was dealing with the effects of the head injury, there would have been no way to do that if I had taken a more traditional job.

There is no way I would ever want to repeat that semester, but I am absolutely positive that I didn't go through it alone.

It didn't take me long to learn that Embry-Riddle was going to be a *lot* more challenging than my previous experiences in college. First off, for the first time ever, I was taking the full-time load of classes. This meant I needed to take at least 12 credits. This wasn't a huge class load, but it was a far cry from the 3 credit hours a semester

I accomplished at Grand Rapids Community College. I was forced to stick with this minimum due to the limitations of my head injury. In comparison, engineering degrees generally require a 14-18 credit hour class load. Even with this load, engineers generally take five years to graduate. At the time, I wasn't the best in math, but even I could see that I was in this for the long haul.

I was doing the best I could to keep up with the classes. But I also had to figure out how to work with my head injury. The classes were hard. The living was harder. As a result, I came close to failing most of my classes. I also ended up doing miserably on that basic math for aviators class. And it had nothing to do with the class being hard, but everything to do with the class being at 7:30 in the morning and me not always being able to get there.

The silver lining of the whole semester was that I didn't lose hope. I felt like I had made some really good friends, and I still felt like I was on the right path through the maze. So, I kept on going.

The spring semester at Embry-Riddle started out much better than the first. It was only a short time after Christmas break that one of those new friends, one of my fraternity brothers, helped fix my car.

Spring semester meant that Daytona Beach was going to be bustling with tourists. This meant there were opportunities for higher paying jobs. At the time, I was making minimum wage at the school. This was an easy job, and the hours were very flexible, but it was all too tempting to take a higher paying job working at the Daytona 500. This job was advertised all around the school, and it involved selling popcorn, peanuts, and drinks to people in the bleachers. So, to me, this meant a chance to make money while watching the world-renowned Daytona 500.

I was oblivious to the fact that I would be in a screaming crowd of drunk and hungry people who were sitting in the hot sun on metal bleachers. Instead of taking the time to watch the race, I would be running up and down the bleachers as quickly as I could with little chance for a break. The blessing in disguise came about a week before the race. I got a shooting pain in one of my eyes. I had no idea why, but a day or so later, I was barely able to open that eye. Not long after, I wasn't able to open the other one either. As it turned out, I was forced to miss my debut at the Daytona 500 due to a bad case of pink eye.

For a while, I continued to go to class like nothing was wrong, but not long after, I went to class wearing sun glasses because the fluorescent lights were too bright. I finally got in to see the optometrist who gave me some eye drops to take care of the pink eye, but it took a couple of weeks before I could return to class.

About this time, I began to feel like the world and God Himself was against me. I had spent most of the first semester without a car, but I wasn't able to recognize how blessed I was to have friends there to help me out. I didn't recognize the lesson I was being taught about the fact that we are all in this ordeal we call life together. I also didn't recognize that, against all probability, the timing belt on my car failed in such a way that it didn't cause me to lose the entire engine. Nor did I recognize that God had led me to a friend that was able to fix my car for me, and all it cost me was a couple of Saturday afternoons and a case of beer.

During the spring semester, all I saw was that I was singled out to come down with a bad case of pink eye. Yet no one else around me seemed to have the same condition. I was so distraught about totally missing the opportunity to work at the Daytona 500 that I neglected to realize the true reality of that working environment and what it would have done to me. Even without having to deal with the results of the head injury, spending all day in the sun running up and down bleachers to sell popcorn and candy could have very easily ended with me in the hospital. Looking back on my ordeals, I have to wonder, was I really being cursed by God or were these experiences really a blessing in disguise?

"I know God will not give me anything I can't handle. I just wish that he didn't trust me so much." – Blessed Teresa of Calcutta.

The unfortunate result of it all was that my grades that first year suffered immensely. I had tremendous trouble concentrating because of the head injury. This meant I would remember very little when sitting in my classes. By the time the spring semester finished, I was just trying to hold on. In spite of all my best efforts, to say that my first year at Embry-Riddle Aeronautical University went badly would be a drastic understatement. After only two semesters at Embry-Riddle, I was put on academic suspension, and I went back to Michigan with my hopes deflated.

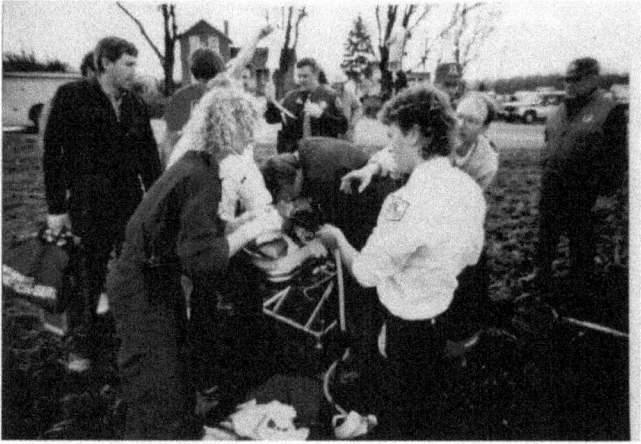

Figure 1 - Actual first responder picture from the accident.

Figure 2 - Aero Med Helicopter (Not actual accident footage)

Figure 3 - Post-Accident Truck Photo (1 of 3)

Figure 4 - Post-Accident Truck Photo (2 of 3)

Figure 5 - Post-Accident Truck Photo (3 of 3)

Figure 6 - Welcome Home From Hospital Party for Ed

Figure 7 - Ed & Char Meek High School Graduation

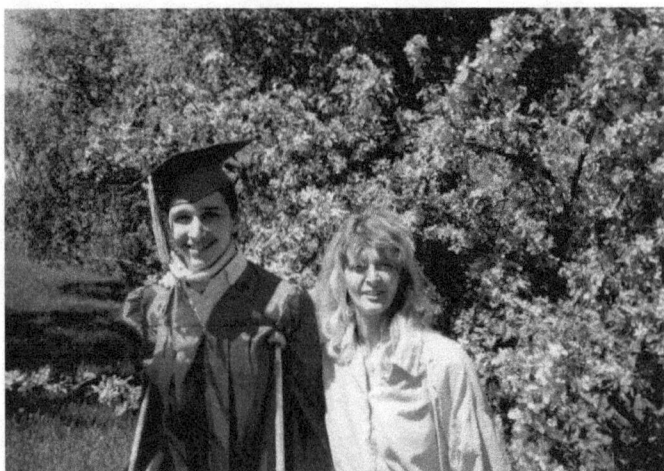

Figure 8 - Ed & Char Meek after High School Graduation

Figure 9 - Christine & Ed Meek after Master's Graduation

Figure 10 - Left To Right – Hunter, David, Taran, and Ed
Meek. Hunter is holding David Meek's Journal from the
accident which he still carries around with him to this day.

Figure 11 - The view from the office where Ed worked while at Kennedy Space Center.

Figure 12 - Left To Right – Orion Project Achievement award following launch and return of EFT-1, NASA impact coin given to Ed by the director of NASA IV&V for his impact on the program, GSDO Project Achievement Award for Ed's work on KSC Ground System (A.K.A GSDO)

Figure 13 – Orion Spacecraft after a successful EFT-1 flight – Taken at the Orion employee friends and family day at Lockheed Martin Space Systems Company

Additional Color Pictures can be viewed at the following site:
http://www.ERtotheStars.com/pictures.html

CHAPTER 8

Psalm 73:26 – My flesh and my heart may fail, but God is the strength of my heart and my portion forever.

After my first attempt at going to school turned out to be a failure, I was on that well-traveled road back to Michigan. With a dejected feeling of failure hanging over my head, I moved back in with my parents to try to get my life back on track.

I hadn't totally given up on my dreams of becoming an engineer, but I realized I would probably have to take the scenic route through college. I ended up taking more classes at Grand Rapids Community College, the same college I had left a year earlier. With what little dignity I had left, I enrolled. This time, I resolved to take some of the harder classes I knew would transfer. Somewhere in my mind, I still didn't want to accept that I should shelve all of my dreams because some doctor told me that maybe engineering wasn't in my cards. I couldn't let them get the best of me. I figured if I beat my head against a wall long enough, something was going to give.

Once again, I went to school taking one class at a time, starting with Calculus 1. During this time, I became ambitious and decided to work full time so that I could save up for my next college. This time, I thought I would try my hand at factory work. So, I worked on a manufacturing line as a solder touch-up technician.

During these days, the moment I got out of bed, I had to just put one foot in front of the other. When I made it through the end of the day, I considered it a successful day. I hated my job, and I knew I would never be able to quit going to school. I figured this is what I have to look forward to if I quit school. There was no way I was going to drop out. So, in that respect, the job served its purpose. It kept me working on my dreams.

Don't get me wrong, as far as factory work is concerned, it wasn't an awful job. There were a lot of people there who were very happy with what they were doing. I was just not one of them.

When I was growing up, the focus at the schools I attended was on graduating students so that they could enter the workforce. There was much less focus on the students who were planning to continue their education. As a result, my high school only offered up to Algebra II. Along with this, I had a little bit of chemistry. But the only physics I had learned had come from watching Bugs Bunny. So, when I got to college and saw that the freshman year schedule required taking Calculus 1 along with Calculus based Physics, Chemistry, and so on, I figured that Calculus must be just an extension of Algebra. Well, that isn't the case.

Calculus 1 was very hard. I only took the one class that first semester back in Michigan. But along with that, I was working full time for the first time in my life, and I was still dealing with the ever present effects of my head injury. As a result, the first time I took Calculus 1, it didn't go so well.

Once again, I had to draw on everything I had and re-take the class. The second time I went to take the class, I still struggled and ended up withdrawing from the class. About this time, things weren't looking good for me. I came very close to giving up hope. If it hadn't been for that factory job, I would have most likely given up all together. But the thought of continuing that God-forsaken job for the rest of my years kept me going.

I still dreamt about returning to Embry-Riddle. Although, after my prior experiences, I felt I needed to stay a little closer to home. In the days before the Internet, I spent hours at the local library trying to come up with a solution. I found Central Michigan University, which was only a couple of hours away from my parents. It offered an Electrical Engineering program which could keep me on track with achieving my goals.

Going there would be both practical and personal. On the practical side, it meant I could come home on the weekends and do laundry or raid the fridge if I needed to. On the personal side, it gave me the escape I needed from a lifetime of soldering.

At Embry-Riddle, there was a large emphasis on engineering and aviation. One of the drawbacks of this emphasis was a disproportion ratio of guys to girls—5 to 1. For an eligible bachelor, this wasn't the best scenario for finding a date. Contrary to this, Central Michigan University specialized in teaching, business, and liberal arts degrees. This meant they had a nice 3 to 1 girl to guy ratio. This was icing on the cake for me, and it was something I really looked forward to.

I had a really good feeling about the school. Already, the school was helping me see the value of mathematics, statistics, and probabilities. But the probabilities just weren't in my favor. I was turned down because my grades were too low at Grand Rapids Community College.

That was my low point, but I had made up my mind not to quit, no matter how bad things got. I was determined not to let that car accident, in one fell swoop, take away all my dreams and goals. I had been through so much that I just couldn't give up. I spent a lot of time thinking to myself that I would have been better off not coming out of that accident.

During my outpatient therapy, I was assigned to a psychologist to help me cope with the trauma. Unfortunately for me, this introduced a new type of trauma. They would tell me that there were many other career paths that didn't require as much schooling. They said it would be a good idea for me to just take it slowly and not to be too disappointed if things didn't work out. I couldn't let that get to me. There was always a sense of smugness that I couldn't stand when they would talk to me about going back to school.

"Well, Mr. Meek, what is on your mind today?" they would ask.

"I'm not sure, but I think it would be nice if they got out a couple more of those pieces of asphalt they missed with all those operations," I would respond.

"You don't seem to be in the best of moods today. Is there something you would like to talk about? You aren't still thinking about going back to school already are you? You know we've talked about that already. Maybe you should give yourself some time to think about it. There are lots of trades you could consider that would be a little less stressful. At least you could take some time to think about it."

No! That was not going to happen to me. I always hated the way that they would say "we've" talked about this when, in reality, it was them talking and me sitting there thinking of how slowly the time would tick by during those sessions.

Before the accident, I would have probably given up long before I had gotten to that point. But not now. Neither of my parents went to college, and I was under no obligation to do anything of the sort. My parents even went so far as to tell me after every class I successfully passed, "Look, there is another one you can take credit for! Even if you don't end up graduating, look how many classes you have taken!" At least they were trying to help me.

Being a father now myself, I can't imagine what they must have been going through. First, to see their son of 18 years immobile in a hospital bed with tubes and wires sticking out everywhere, and then when he came back from the dead, he would not accept what had happened to him. Why couldn't he realize how lucky he was to be alive?

But I wasn't lucky to be alive. I was barely alive. I kept thinking that I had another chance at life. I wasn't going to waste it. I only have one chance here on Earth, and I needed to make it count. I knew it wasn't going to be easy. I knew I had every reason to believe I was just going to end up failing again. But I couldn't give up on that hope. I needed to "live" with myself a while longer, and I didn't want to think I had given up. So many times in my life, I have looked back and thought, "Well, if I had only..." or "If it wasn't for...." This was not going to be one of those times. I had been through so much already.

I had read somewhere in the Grand Rapids Community College guides and handbooks that you were allowed to "replace" grades if you took a class twice. But what about if you had taken a class more than twice? Could you replace that grade with x+1's grade? See, I was getting better at math already! I had to find out.

So, I went to the guidance counselor at Grand Rapids Community College and asked if grades were replaced when we retook a class. His condescending response was something along the lines of, "Yes, but you can't retake every class three times and expect to graduate." That cemented the idea that this is MY life and that I was going to LIVE it! I wasn't going to take this counselor's patronizing remarks. I learned from the mistakes I had made at Embry-Riddle. I had learned that guidance counselors are there to help you, but sometimes they don't. In my case, this guidance counselor DID help me, albeit inadvertently. When he told me that, I thanked him for the information, and I told him that I would be back later with a better grade so that he could replace my past grades. In a somewhat polite sense, I told him where he could stick his opinion.

I had gone beyond "pissed off," and I had reached

"determined." I immediately walked over and registered for Calculus 1 for the third time. Then I checked with the bookstore to get the latest book. Once I had the book, I knew I needed to do something different to make it through the class. So, I went in search of a tutor. Unfortunately, there were not many people taking Calculus 1 at Grand Rapids Community College at the time, so tutors were scarce. There was a tutoring session that was held once or twice a week, but I needed to figure out how I could work this extra tutoring into my schedule. I needed to work with their schedule, but I realized that I also needed to work within the limitations imposed on me from my head injury.

There were times of the day that worked better for my concentration. I knew I needed to work within these constraints. So, I made myself a study schedule. And wouldn't you know it, these times were NOT the times that the tutors were offering. So once again, I had to improvise.

I found out that when I worked with the tutors, they would give me the scrap notes that we had gone through. I could go through the scrap notes later when I felt like I had a chance at actually understand what they were trying to tell me. I bought a tape recorder so that I could record the lectures and replay them later as I was going through and trying to decipher what the professor was trying to say as it related to the homework.

At the time, there was a product on the market called "Where There's a Will, There's an A." I had bought this set of audio CDs earlier and had the opportunity to listen to them at work while I was working at my factory job. See, there was a purpose behind another one of my stumbling blocks, and this led me down a future path.

I certainly had the will, so I applied what I had learned from the program. The recommendations from this study help program worked very well for me. They recommended that I needed to take my study sessions in smaller chunks. So instead of working for two hours straight, I would need to set aside three or four hours and work for fifteen minute sessions at a time with small breaks between study sessions. This seemed inefficient. But the point was to learn the material. There was no prize for efficiency or style. I just had to make it work.

I also found out that there was a study guide for the new Calculus book that I had purchased. But the closest place that sold it was at the Michigan State University bookstore in Lansing, Michigan. After finding this out, I went on a road trip and picked it up. I later found out, to my great surprise, that the same book and study guide was used for my Calculus 2 and 3 classes as well. Sometimes the path that I was led down had victories. This was a small victory. But even a small victory helped to ignite that spark of hope I still carried with me.

With this hope, I was driven to try one more possibility. On a whim, I took a day off work and drove up to Central Michigan University. At the university, I talked to the guidance counselors there. I hoped that after talking to me in person they might see the error in their ways. Indeed, they didn't have any idea what my story was. They had rejected my application solely because of how I looked on paper. When I told them what I had been through and that I was not about to let it stop me, I got a firm commitment from them that if I were to get a "B" or better in Calculus 1, then I would be accepted.

Well I did get a "B" or better in calculus that semester. In fact, I got an "A"! In January, I quit my crappy factory job and I moved up to Mount Pleasant, Michigan, and started going to Central Michigan University.

CHAPTER 9

James 1:12 – Blessed is the one who perseveres under trial because, having stood the test, that person will receive the crown of life that the Lord has promised to those who love him.

The first thing I learned at Central Michigan University was that the class of Electrical Engineering students that year was a bit small. By small, I mean there were six of us. I found out that the Electrical Engineering program there at the time was really created to bring students from around the farmlands in the central Michigan region up to Michigan Tech in Houghton, Michigan. The program was created so that high school graduates could easily take classes close to home and then transfer up to Michigan Tech where they would complete their last two years of college.

The size of the class wasn't really a problem for me; the problem came when I went to find a tutor. Learning from my previous experiences, I wanted to get all the help I could early on in the semester. Head injury or not, it's a good idea. Although the engineering program was small, the university also had a physics and chemistry department, so I thought they would know where I could get help. However, when I went in to the Physics Department to ask about tutors for the calculus based physics class, the response was, "You know calculus? Would you like a job?" So I was hired by Central Michigan University as a calculus and physics tutor.

Ironic as it seems, being a tutor and getting paid to help people learn calculus and physics was better than getting a tutor for myself. In order to teach something, you really have to learn it yourself first.

So, by trying to break down how derivatives worked physically so that I could explain it to others, I helped myself to understand it better. Aside from that, I was working alongside physics experts who really understood the physics, but didn't have any idea how to model those physical things mathematically. I learned a lot more about physics that first year than I had ever learned in my life, and I wouldn't have ever grasped those abstract concepts if I had not tried to teach them to someone else. Sometimes, when you come upon obstacles, you have to rise about those limitations and make your own way around them. It worked for me.

Overall, my first semester at Central Michigan University went very well. I lived on campus (having learned from a previous mistake), and I also had a limited meal plan at the cafeteria which ensured that I had something to eat for at least one meal a day.

The semester was still stressful, but I got to learn a lot about myself and how I was able to handle stress. I also worked hard at finding ways to eliminate as much stress as possible. One of the most effective ways was to go to class, but not go to *my* classes. I found it quite fun to go to other people's classes. This was especially the case when the class was on a topic I was interested in and it was a high-level class. I called these my "anti-classes." This might sound really strange, but let me walk you through one of my more vivid experiences.

I was always a bit fascinated with how the brain works, and after sitting for hours listening to psychologists say stuff like, "Hmmm...so how did that make you feel?", I was even more intrigued. When I had a friend tell me that she was taking a high-level psychology class that was going to have a series of lectures on dreams, it was an opportunity I didn't want to pass up.

I asked my friend, "Could I tag along when you go to

your psychology class?"

She responded, "Why on Earth would you want to do something like that?"

In a joking manner, I said, "I could really use another hour or so of sleep."

She thought it funny, so she brought me along. Her class was in one of those really big lecture halls, the type portrayed in movies and on television shows. Just like in these shows, it had probably close to 150 seats by my best estimate. The seats were all arranged auditorium style with the entrances near the top on the very back. Down at the bottom of the auditorium were a set of white boards. I remember these explicitly, because many of my classes were held in the same sort of forum, but my professors seemed to be all old school as they were still using chalk boards. By the end of my classes, the professors were always covered in a thin layer of white chalk dust. I imagined that this professor didn't have the same sort of problem.

When I saw the enormity of the lecture hall, I thought there wouldn't be any problem with me blending in with the rest of the students. I was a bit surprised when only about half of the auditorium filled up. This didn't turn out to be any sort of a problem though as I ended up actually attending several of those classes that semester. If the professor did recognize that I wasn't one of his students, he at least had the decency not to point me out. It was either that or he was just happy to see one more of those seats filled.

I quickly found out that I really didn't have a clue what the professor was talking about. There wasn't any of that "Hmmm...I see..." or "How does that make you feel?" business going on. I learned that there was actually quite a bit of schooling behind each of those "Hmmm's." It at least helped me to realize that my psychologists probably did have some understanding and probably had my best interest in mind. I found out that psychology is really complicated. It wasn't a problem for me since I was only along for the ride. It didn't matter one bit to me how much homework the professor assigned. I wasn't going to do it! Of course, I wasn't expected to do any work. I wasn't even expected to be there. But each time I went to one of these anti-classes, it had the effect of releasing a little bit of that pressure that had been building up inside of me. This was my version of screaming at the top of my lungs, because I didn't know what else I could do.

I had a lot of fun that first day, and I went back a few more times. One of the best feelings (for me) was having the professor say, "Now don't forget about the test we have coming up on Monday. To help you prepare for it, you should read chapter 17 sections 11-19." I usually sat in the back to better blend in, and I could just see everyone's shoulders drop when they heard this. I also heard a scattering of, "Oh man!" I know it was probably not good of me to be relieving stress by watching the stress of others, but I needed something to help me release some of that stress! If you ever have the opportunity, I would highly recommend it.

The semester eventually ended, and I was back home for the summer. After all I had been through, the successful completion of this first semester represented a much needed success for me. I was not yet a stellar student by any means, but I had managed to get through the semester with a passing grade for all classes. At this point in my life, it was important to claim victory where I could, no matter how small.

CHAPTER 10

Genesis 2:18 – The Lord God said, "It is not good for the man to be alone. I will make him a helper suitable for him.

When fall came, I found myself back at Central Michigan University. This time, I was in it for my first full year, and things were going well for me as a student. I decided to live off campus, but this time I made sure my new apartment was well within walking distance. I also maintained my one meal a day ticket to the dining hall. I made sure to learn from previous mistakes as well as successes.

Better yet, I found a set of music rooms that were set up for music appreciation classes. These were little rooms about the size of a large closet or a very small room. There was a set of four of them all against one wall of a larger room that looked very much like a library. These music rooms each had their own door, which meant that they were each stand-alone enclosures. If you have ever seen a recording studio with the glass wall that looks into a sound room where the musicians are supposed to perform, then you would have some idea of how these rooms looked. Only these rooms were smaller and there was only room for a medium size adult to stretch out lengthwise across the floor.

At one end of the rooms, an attendant sat at a desk. The attendant controlled a stereo system which piped music to each of the enclosures. The purpose of these rooms was to provide a catalog of various music that an occupant could listen to. In fact, each of them had a set of cushions covering the floor. You could reserve these rooms for a couple of hours and just go in and lay down on the cushions and listen to music. In my case, these were centrally located on campus, so I could go in and take a nap when I needed. It was the perfect setup for me as I was still dealing with the aftereffects of my head injury. I never did take the music appreciation class, but I certainly did appreciate the music.

In October, some friends invited me over to their dorm room for an impromptu week-night party. This was the kind of thing that I usually avoided, because I normally had classes on Friday. But I didn't have any studying to do that night, which was a big thing for me, so I decided to go with them. Along the way, they met a girl they knew, Bonnie, and stopped to chat with her. I did something out of character for me; I invited Bonnie along to the party so that I would have someone to talk to. She agreed, and we brought her along to the party with us.

During the event, we all got hungry, so we decided to order a pizza. My friend Jeff picked up the phone to call it in, but it was the hand of God that dialed the wrong number and ended up calling the front desk of one of the dorms.

By this time, Bonnie was most of the way through one bottle of wine and was talking quite loudly. It was then that the girl at the other end of the wrong number recognized Bonnie's voice. Ironically enough, Bonnie had gone to middle school with the unlikely receptionist, but they hadn't seen each other since then. After a little coaxing, Christine, who was the receptionist, decided to come join our impromptu soiree.

That night was a memorable turning point in my life. I didn't realize it at the time, but the events of that night started me down a path where I met my best friend and future wife. As it turned out, I never saw Bonnie again, because when the party finished, we went our separate ways. But because of a wrong number and a loud date, Christine joined our little group of friends.

Yet again, I had borne witness to another miracle. My night had started out with an out of character decision to attend an impromptu party. Along the way, I had a chance meeting with a perfect stranger who I, at the last minute, decided to ask out on a date. During that party, a wrong number led to an amazing reunion and us meeting. In the 20 plus years since then, I have come to know that her decision to join the party was also very out of character for Christine. It sounds like something out of a Harlequin romance novel. But it happened to me.

That was the way my relationship with Christine started. Christine is now my wife of over 20 years. To me, this is not only proof that there is a God, but it also shows that if it is His will, even a series of what seems like random and unlikely events will bring two people together.

That night was the beginning of a beautiful relationship. Over a period of six months or so, Christine and I became close friends. Eventually, we started dating. I hope that we never stop.

For over two and a half years after that, Christine and I went on many adventures, canoeing, hiking, and just spending time together. Since we were both poor college students and had very little money, our favorite date was to take $5 for a loaf of bread and some cheese. Then we would take our picnic to our special spot where we would often watch the sunset. Since sunset was the time of my accident, I was very uncomfortable driving at that time. The light plays tricks on me, and I cannot trust what I see or what I don't see. So those were the times when Christine drove. She always takes the wheel when I can't. There are other times when I do likewise. To me, it is a match made in heaven.

CHAPTER 11

2 Corinthians 8:11 – Now finish the work, so that your eager willingness to do it may be matched by your completion of it, according to your means.

By the summer of 1995, I finally felt like the worst was behind me. I finished up all the classes I could take at Central Michigan University, and I was working full time at a pharmaceutical plant in Zeeland, Michigan. After the summer was over, they even asked me to stay with them full time as a systems engineer. I eagerly took this position as it meant an opportunity to actually work as a real engineer, and I hadn't even gotten my degree yet.

Eventually though, it came time for Christine to graduate. Along with Christine graduating, we wanted to get married. So it was also another point in my life when I had to make a hard decision. At work, I was a true engineer. My official title said "Systems Engineer," and I had the business cards to prove it. But I did not have an engineering degree or a degree of any kind. I was planning on getting married and having kids. But I knew that if I were to somehow lose my job, I would not have that degree to help me to get a new job.

So I made the decision to quit and go back to school to finish my degree. At Central Michigan University I brought my grades up so I had confidence that I would be accepted at the Embry-Riddle campus in Arizona. I had always dreamed of working in aerospace, and I figured that going back to an aeronautical university would give me the contacts I needed within the Aerospace community. That, and I really didn't want to go to Michigan Tech – the school where you needed to take a snowmobile to class most of the winter. I could finish up my degree in electrical engineering and have some sort of assurance in any job. Christine and I were still dating, and we made the decision to get married and move out to Arizona together.

At the time, I felt like this time I could actually see my path before me. I knew in my heart that it was going to be all right. So, although I was now responsible for two lives, I took yet another leap of faith, knowing it would be different this time.

CHAPTER 12

Ecclesiastes 4:9-12 – Two are better than one, because they have a good return for their labor: If either of them falls down, one can help the other up. But pity anyone who falls and has no one to help them up. Also, if two lie down together, they will keep warm. But how can one keep warm alone? Though one may be overpowered, two can defend themselves.

On August 9, 1996, after working a great job for more than a year, I quit. Quitting the job this time it was much harder as I not only left behind a position I had grown to love, but I had made many friends there. On August 10, 1996, I got married to Christine in Battle Creek, Michigan. On August 11, 1996, I hopped on a moving van and moved my new bride across the country to Prescott, Arizona.

In Prescott, Arizona, Christine and I got to start our new life away from friends, family, and everything we knew. The only thing that followed us out there were my crappy grades from Embry-Riddle Aeronautical University in Daytona Beach from back in 1991.

As it turns out, grades from other Universities were not transferable. So, all of the good grades I had gotten at Grand Rapids Community College and Central Michigan University didn't count. I only got credit for all the classes. But because both the Prescott, AZ, and Daytona Beach, FL, campuses were part of Embry-Riddle, I got to keep my permanent grade record. To this day, I have a minor in mathematics which means I took a good number of classes in this subject area. In my case, I had over 18 credit hours, not including the basic math class. I have taken calculus 1, 2, and 3, linear algebra, advanced engineering mathematics, and differential equations. But I have a "D" in MA-111 which is basic mathematics. I like to think of this as my true measure of how far I have come.

It had been over a year since I was in college, and once again, going to back to school was really hard. When I was working as an engineer, I had very minimal problems with the aftereffects of the head injury. But going back to school was very different. Stress and lack of sleep seemed to amplify the effects of the head injury. It was really all I could do to get through school. Luckily, this time, I had brought along my best friend.

In order to make it through the classes, I would go to school at 7:00 a.m. and come home sometime around 11:00 p.m. I still needed to nap in the afternoons, but not as often. I needed to study more than others, so I gathered a group of friends to help me out. I was given a key to the engineering building so I could let me and my study group in and out after hours. We used to have a saying, "cooperate to graduate."

Don't get me wrong; it wasn't like we would cheat on each other's tests or anything. I don't think it is even feasible to cheat on a test when you have only two questions and each answer requires a page and a half of calculations. It was more like a support group. We would spend hours in front of a white board drawing pictures and writing equations. Really, when I think about it, not much has changed with what I do now at work, but at least now I get paid for it.

Overall, though, there is a sense of comradery that you develop with your classmates. I graduated from a class of 15 electrical engineers. I still keep in touch with most of them through Facebook. We worked hard, but then we would play hard too. There is just something about pushing through the hard times with someone that gives you a special relationship. That is what my wife and I have. That is why I believe we are still together. It takes a good forge and lots of hammering to make a strong sword. Like it or not, sometimes you need to persevere through the hammering to become the instrument that God wants you to be.

Christine supported me through our time in Prescott, not just emotionally, but financially and personally at home too. The days were long and lonely for her while I was at school. I would come home for an hour or so in the evening to eat dinner, but then I went back to the school to study. Even though she had a college degree, she could only find a job that paid just over minimum wage. In some ways, it was good to go to school in that small town, but when it came to the job market, Prescott was certainly lacking.

Christine worked at a historic hotel downtown, as a real estate appraiser, as a barista for a coffee shop, and finally as a computer trainer for a local computer dealer. At one point, we figured out that if we were going to stay off welfare we needed to get creative. But, thanks to Christine, we did get creative and never asked for governmental assistance.

We ate nothing but frozen pizzas for months on end, and we made it through together. On top of working full time, Christine had to do all the cooking, cleaning, and pay the bills. I just was not able to spare any energy outside of school. Engineering is a difficult degree for anyone, but for someone with a head injury, it was especially hard.

During the summers, when I didn't have class, we started our own computer consulting company. We designed web pages together; she would help train clients on the software, and I would help them with hardware. We were and still are the perfect team.

With a lot of work between us, I graduated with a bachelor's degree in electrical engineering with minor in computer science and mathematics in the summer of 1998. It was fully 9 years after I had started, but I made it nonetheless.

CHAPTER 13

Hebrews 10:36 – You need to persevere so that when you have done the will of God, you will receive what he has promised.

After graduating from Embry-Riddle, I was finally working as a true engineer, and it was everything I hoped it would be. I started out in the aerospace industry, and I did pretty well. Initially, I worked on the software for aircraft flight control systems. I worked at a couple of different large aerospace corporations, and I enjoyed being an engineer more than ever. Eventually, I was promoted, and I became the systems and test engineering lead for a large aircraft program doing a flight management systems software upgrade. I managed to participate in several flight tests. This had been a lifelong dream of mine. I had finally made it!

During these years, Christine and I started growing our family. We now have our two boys. They are the joy of my life, and I have so much fun with them and watching them grow up. We moved around the country a few times as I went from one contract to another, from one employer to another. They have supported me in every move, and I am forever grateful.

Eventually, the door of opportunity opened again, and I took one more step in the maze that led me to where I am today. That was when I was offered a job working on space systems.

Working on space systems was on a whole different world from the aircraft systems, quite literally. My new job dealt with satellite operations, and although I was still considered a systems engineer, my job title was a combination of an orbital analyst and mission analyst.

Without getting into too much detail, an orbital analyst tells you where a satellite is going to go, and a mission analyst tells it what to do when it gets there. It was extremely exciting. Only this was totally different than anything I had ever done, so it wasn't too long until I was thinking about going back to school for a master's degree.

If you would have told me when I was going for my bachelor's degree that I would someday be going back to get my master's degree, I would have thought you were crazy. If you would have told me at that time that I would be going back to Embry-Riddle for my masters, I would have laughed at you. But our God works in mysterious ways.

It just so happened that, after I decided to go back to school to learn more about my new career, several of the people I was working with started going to school at Embry-Riddle Worldwide Campus that is both on the Internet and at other locations around the world, including Albuquerque, New Mexico, which is where I was living at the time.

I was working full time and going to school full time at Embry-Riddle for my masters. It helped me significantly because I was going to school for something that I was interested in and it was already a field I was working in. I learned about the laws of astrodynamics and really enjoyed what I was doing both in school and at work.

At home, my wife, Christine, took care of everything. Although the accident was almost barely a memory, I must admit I still had limitations. Working full time and going to graduate school full time left me with no energy to do anything else. She cooked, cleaned, paid the bills, and stayed at home with our two toddler boys. When I got home from work, I would sit on the couch and stare at the television for hours until it was time to gather any strength I had left and study. She would put the boys to bed and be sure I said goodnight to them. She made sure I was present in their lives as much as I could be. On Saturdays, I slept until 10, would study for a couple of hours, take a nap, and finally, about 5 p.m., I would be able to be involved with my family. Christine's strength and hard work at home made it possible for me to succeed at school and work.

When it came time to work on my final graduate research project, I decided I would go as far as I could. Once again, I went down the path less traveled. Everything pointed to me that I should do this. Yes, the hand of God was steering me once again.

I was working as an orbital analyst on systems that I thought were really interesting. This was my opportunity to learn more about what I was already working on. It sounded like more work. But at the same time, it was more work that I was uniquely qualified to do because of the path I had been led down. It was also more work that I felt I would enjoy.

Sometimes, those indicators that tell which path to take are barely whispering, and it is hard to tell for sure which path to take. I have no doubt that I could have chosen the other path, and my life would have worked out just fine. But I know Who is guiding me. What's more, I trust Him.

I have had times when I have tried to choose the wrong path. The reason I know it was the wrong path is because I constantly felt like a salmon swimming upstream. Eventually, I would end up getting back on the path God had planned for me, but looking back, I can often see how it would have been so much easier if I would have taken the other path in the first place! I wish I could expound on that more. But it is just a feeling, similar to the one you get when you are doing something wrong and knowing it is wrong. Conversely, it is like the feeling you get when you do something because it is "the right thing to do." There has never been a glaring sign saying, "This way" or "Caution, dead end." I have always just needed to pray on it and look into my heart and try to understand which way it was telling me to go.

During a difficult time in my life, I had a friend that said, "Don't worry, Ed, cream floats." What I interpreted that to mean is that things will come out all right in the end. At the time, I was worried about taking a test the next day, which I subsequently failed miserably, so I assumed he was a raging lunatic. But now it somehow makes more sense. Don't sweat the small stuff. Eventually, it all works out the way it is supposed to. God's got your back. Those are probably good words to live by.

Either way, I chose to do a master's thesis rather than the standard graduate research project. The differences between the master's thesis and a graduate research project can be substantial. In my case, the thesis was much more technical than required by the graduate research project. It also required more expert reviewers, but it also sounded like a whole lot more fun to me, and I needed to prove to myself that I could do it.

Once again, my goal was met with resistance by others. This time, instead of a guidance counselor, it was the department chair for the program. I found out that I was only the second person to attempt a master's thesis in all the years that the facility had been there, and the last thesis had been done over 10 years prior by someone who worked at Sandia Labs, which is where the elite work. I was basically told I wasn't elite enough or capable enough to do a thesis. When I heard this, I was once again driven to challenge the status quo. This time, it wasn't as hard.

When I brought my proposal to the department chair, she listened very hard to my arguments. In the end though, she said, "Congratulations, you're doing a thesis." I've learned that sometimes naysayers really do want to see you succeed; you just need to show them that you are willing to work for it.

From that moment on, the department chair along with one of the adjunct professors at the time were two of my biggest supporters. That adjunct professor even brought to my attention a grant proposal that was being offered by the school to help fund different research topics. I applied for this grant and was accepted.

In the end, I graduated after two years with my master's degree in aeronautical science with a specialization in space studies. My master's thesis, which is titled "A Comparison of Orbit Rendezvous Routines for Satellites Flying in Low Earth Orbit" has been published on Amazon, the internet shopping company, in 2013.

In December, 2006, I graduated Summa Cum Laude with a 4.0 grade point average. Believe it or not, I finally got past that stupid math grade that plagued me for so long! As it turns out, when I started my master's program, no grades were brought in from my bachelor's program, although it was still technically the same school.

For me, the culmination of what was, at that point, a 19-year struggle came just after I graduated with my master's degree. A couple of paragraphs back, I mentioned that I had been awarded a research grant from Embry-Riddle. Well, as part of that grant, I was also awarded the opportunity to come down to Embry-Riddle's main campus in Daytona Beach, Florida, to present my work to the ERAU Board of Directors. So, in 2007, I flew to Daytona Beach, Florida. Yes, it is the same Embry-Riddle that I failed out of in 1991. It was also the same Embry-Riddle that didn't accept my application to Aeronautical Engineering when I applied before graduating high school in 1989. As a matter of fact, this was the first time I had been back there since I had left in 1991.

To recap, I had managed to graduate with my bachelor's degree in electrical engineering in 1998 after 9 years of hardship. This could have easily been the end of my story. But it wasn't, and I was led back to the school that had proven to be my nemesis for so many years before. But this time, I was given a fresh start. Against all odds, I was led to not only graduate, but also present my work to those who had so many years prior turned down my admission to the school for the degree program of my choice.

At no point was a looking for revenge. I was not even looking for retribution. What I was looking for was the chance to prove to myself that I could do it. I wanted to prove to myself that I could achieve my goal of graduating with my master's degree. I had been the first one in my immediate family to graduate college. But for me, this was just what I had felt I needed to do. This was my path down my maze.

All those years of hardship had left me crushed and broken. But I still had my hope. I had worked so hard only to have just "graduated." I had been fighting a severe head injury, and it should have been enough for me to know that I had made it. But it wasn't.

I think that God, my "Maze Master," must have known this, and He led me down the path less taken. He had led me to that place where I had a chance to show to myself and to those who I felt had opposed me what I was capable of. But I didn't do this on my own. I fully acknowledge that it was only with God's help that I accomplished more than I had ever dreamed I would.

The defining moment came when I presented my master's work to that board of directors for Embry-Riddle. They looked at what I presented with fascination. In the end, they gave me a standing ovation. No, I didn't want revenge. I wanted approval. That is what I got. Praise God.

CHAPTER 14

Jeremiah 29:11 – "For I know the plans I have for you," declares the Lord, "plans to prosper you and not to harm you, plans to give you hope and a future."

As of this writing, it has been over 25 years of trials, tribulations, and recovery after a severe head injury. It was an incredible journey, but I finally made it to where I always wanted to be. I have earned both my bachelor's and master's degrees. I have become somewhat of an expert for spacecraft navigation (by all definitions, a true rocket scientist). I have worked with NASA doing independent verification and validation. My first job with NASA IV&V was doing verification of the software for a new ground system at Kennedy Space Center (KSC). Yes, working at KSC was even more exciting than I had dreamed. Looking at it from the outside, you really can't appreciate the immense size of the facilities and the buildings. It was incredible. I saw firsthand where all that history took place.

Although I loved every minute that I worked on the KSC ground systems, eventually I was offered a position I couldn't refuse. I was offered the lead analyst position for the team doing the independent verification and validation for NASA's Orion program. Orion is the future of NASA's human space flight, and I am one of the people ensuring that it is safe for humans to fly. It is truly awe-inspiring to think that, in a way, I am helping to shape new history.

To say that my path was not easy would be a drastic understatement. But without that path, I would not be the person who I am today. I thank God every day for the path He has led me down. It was a path that is full of hardships, but it also had its share of blessings. Yes, I actually do thank God for those hardships. They were indicators that steered me in the right direction.

I no longer wonder why the accident happened to me. I am glad I went through all I did. This might sound strange, but I think sometimes we need either a swift kick in the pants or to get whacked upside the head. In my case, that was quite literal. Without those doctors to tell me what I "couldn't do," I know I would have eventually given up on going to college and becoming an engineer. I was raised in a small rural farming community where none of my friends went to college, and even my parents didn't expect me to go. I truly believe I needed a good whack up the side of my head to keep me going. I needed someone to piss me off right down to my very core. That was the only way. That is where my maze has led me so far. I look forward with trepidation, but also with anticipation, to what lies ahead.

For those of you who may have lost hope somewhere along the way, I am living proof that dreams can be achieved. Always remember, the things you face right now might seem insurmountable. But these may turn out to be blessings in disguise as they may be setting you up for future successes. There is life after a severe head injury or whatever problem it is you face.

What I went through to get to where I am has been hard. There were many days when I came very close to quitting. But then where do you go once you quit? You still wake up in the same body and you still must live with yourself. There were many times I wondered why this had to happen to me. There were also many times when I just had to stop questioning why I was still working toward this unachievable goal. After a while, it just becomes what you do. You just get up in the morning (or afternoon) and go to another class. I did it, because I couldn't see myself not doing it. I guess in some ways that might seem like a dismal way of working toward a goal. But it is what I had to do. The one thing I never lost is hope. I hope I never do.

The story you just read was written from my (Ed's) perspective. But my experience touched the lives of my whole family. On the following pages is the story written from their perspectives.

A Mother's Perspective

Char Meek

As of this writing, it's been twenty-three and a half years since Ed's accident, and even now, I find it very hard to think about. Over time, I've managed to block things out and forget many of the details I really should be able to remember. Yet, there are moments that are as clear today as they were 23 years ago—things I will NEVER forget. I suppose, this is why it's so hard to write about the accident. It forces me to be face to face with something too painful to relive.

It was a mother's worst nightmare, that evening of April 4, 1989—the sirens, the sound of the helicopter, the sheriff's patrol car sitting in the driveway. It was around 6:00 p.m. when Ed got ready to leave for work at the theater in Holland, about a twenty-minute drive from our house. His small compact car wouldn't start, so he asked his dad if he could use the pickup truck, a full-size Dodge with a camper shell on the back. Had he been in his car, there is no doubt in my mind that he wouldn't have lived.

But, in order to do all this justice, I need to take you back exactly one year and one week earlier to another nightmare and another child. On that particular night, our daughter, Wendy, was involved in a serious car accident about two and a half miles from our house. It was a single car rollover. The driver was going way too fast to negotiate the curve. My daughter and her boyfriend were in the back seat. Both were thrown from the car. She landed in the middle of the road, he, in the adjacent corn field. The other passenger in the front seat was in very serious condition and later died in the ER.

After that night, sirens became a constant source of fear for me. Hearing any sirens, at any time, would cause an immediate panic. I would mentally wonder where my two teens were and if they were safe. Often, I would have to fight the urge to follow the sirens to their destination. And when I heard the sirens on the night of Ed's accident, I had to fight the urge to run out of my house and follow them. I am forever thankful that I never followed through on that urge. Because of the almost 90-degree angle curve in the road where our daughter's accident occurred and the very bad intersection where Ed's accident happened, sirens happened frequently, unusual for a rural area.

But it was on the anniversary of our daughter's accident that I remember the most. I had a conversation with the mother of Wendy's boyfriend who had also been hurt. She said to me, "It's one thing to get a phone call from the hospital saying your child has been in an accident, but it's an entirely different thing to have a policeman knocking on your door." It was this conversation I remembered as I looked out the window to find the sheriff's car in our driveway.

So, Ed left for work. It seemed only moments later when I heard the sirens and then the sound of a helicopter overhead. Immediately, I knew...I just knew. There wasn't any doubt in my mind that it was Ed. I was in a panic state. I remember going upstairs three steps at a time, trying to find my husband. I screamed at him, "It's Ed! I know it's Ed!" Then I looked out the window and there, in the driveway, was the sheriff's car. I had an instant flash back to that conversation just one week prior.

Almost at the same time, a knock on my door heralded the news I knew was coming. The sheriff stood on our doorstep and told me our son was involved in an accident and was being medivacked to Butterworth Hospital, a trauma center in Grand Rapids, about a 20-minute drive away. I asked about Ed, but he just told me, "All I can tell you is you need to get to the hospital right away."

I don't remember the drive to the hospital, but what stood out significantly was what happened when we got there. Immediately, we were ushered into a "room" and were met with counselors or hospital staff trained to "comfort and console," but also trained to not give you any real answers.

I had another flashback of a year before. At that time, we had been taken straight into the ER to see our daughter. But this was different. I don't remember breathing. They told us Ed was alive and that he was being "worked on." No, we couldn't see him, but they'd let us know when we could. I don't remember how long we were in that room. Time, for me, stopped.

I remember making two phone calls, one to our church and another to my friend. It wasn't long before the youth pastor arrived. He was our salvation. He was able to go in and out of the emergency room where Ed was being worked on. He was able to give us an honest update as time passed. Without him, we would've been so very lost and alone.

I have no concept of time during our stay there. I know that it was a long night. I know it was around 6:00 p.m. at the time of the accident. I'm not sure when we were finally allowed to see him. It seemed like forever, but I know we were allowed only a brief visit.

He was sitting semi reclined in the typical ER bed. The doctors and nurses surrounded him. Someone was stitching up his face and the cuts next to his eye. He wore a neck brace and another contraption protruded from his mouth. Someone else was pumping air from this balloon-like thing through the tube in his mouth.

Another flashback.

A year before in the ER with our daughter, I saw this very same procedure being done to the passenger who had been in the front seat of the car. Air was being pumped into his lungs, trying to keep him alive. He didn't make it. He died in the ER.

So suddenly, I'm watching all this happening to my son! "Lord! He's only eighteen years old...please don't take my son!"

We were told his leg was badly broken and that two of his vertebrae in his upper neck were going to have to be fused together. His spinal cord came that close to being severed. They mentioned a closed head injury and a pelvic injury. I could hear the doctors talking, but I felt like I was in an echo chamber, like their words were way off in the distance and were being drowned out by the beating of my heart and by the sound of my own breathing. No one could give us a prognosis. All we were told was that "The first 24 hours are critical."

I don't know when he was finally moved to a room. I remember it was a private room. I was thankful for that. I remember his eyes were closed. He laid there very still. I'd call his name, and he'd open his eyes briefly, and then they'd droop close again. This became a routine. I'd call his name, his eyes would open, and then he'd close them. He was alive...semi-conscious, but alive. It was something I could hold on to. It was hope. I don't remember when we left the hospital. I don't remember going home. It was just so very important to me that we not leave him.

As the days progressed, the doctors, doing what they do best, filled our minds with words like, "We don't know to what extent the closed head injury will have on Ed's future. He may never return to normal. He may need permanent care. His short-term memory could be severely affected. His writing and motor skills may never return to normal." The nurses weren't any better. One nurse told us it was too early to tell if there would be permanent brain damage.

I just wanted to scream at them to just get away from my son with all that negative talk! I thought, *If we all listened to you, he doesn't stand a chance!* I choose to believe that God saved him for a purpose and that God was in control of his present and his future. I wish I would've had the courage to tell the doctors and nurses this. I guess a person looks to them as authority figures, but this doom and gloom approach could severely affect the outcome of a person's life. Fortunately, my son did not fall into that category.

On April 6, just two days after the accident, Ed underwent surgery from 12:30 till 7:30 p.m. The two vertebrae were fused together in his neck to give it more stability and ward off any chance of damaging the spinal cord. Additional surgery was done on his pelvis and his leg. A stainless steel rod and pins were inserted to hold his leg together. It would be a year or two down the road when he would undergo further surgery to have them removed. But there was nothing they could do for the closed head injury. Only time would tell. It takes time and lots of rest for the brain to heal. It's like a large bowl of Jell-O that shifted during impact. There were no answers.

Ed slept most of the time during the days ahead. He remained in intensive care for three days. Life, as I knew it, stopped. I was a salesperson for a printing company. A week before the accident, I was approached by the owner of another printing company to join his team. I graciously accepted his offer and was waiting for the right moment to give my two weeks' notice. This seemed like the right moment. I cleaned out my desk, grabbed my files, and left. But, at that point, I didn't think I'd ever be working again. My son needed fulltime care or at least that's what I imagined the outcome to be. Nothing else mattered.

The days ahead became a blur. So many details are so vague. I don't know when he finally awoke enough to talk. I just remember the smallest things tiring him out. They said his brain was like a computer. When it gets overloaded, it shuts down. No amount of trying could revive it. It takes rest...lots of rest.

Emotions are strange things. Emotions can hold you captive for years, even though you don't realize it, or, if faced, they can set you free from the shadows that lurk in the deepest recesses of the mind. The concept of time means nothing. Twenty-three years vanish in a brief moment of a breath...so many details lost...others run together like a bad dream.

As his physical injuries began to heal, it became apparent that the next step to his recovery was rehabilitation. Fortunately for us, Grand Rapids housed one of the leading hospitals for occupational and physical therapy, Mary Free Bed (MFB). So, after being a patient at Butterworth Hospital for around three weeks, Ed was transferred to this rehab hospital as an in-patient. No answers were given as to how long he'd be there, but I knew he was in the best place, receiving the best of care.

Physical injuries can heal. My main concern was for his memory loss and his loss of motor skills, and it was MFB's job to help him in every way possible. It was their job to push him beyond his physical and mental limits. This would take time. This would not be an easy road for him.

Brain overload and computer shut down became a way of life. He needed so much rest. Constant fatigue walked beside him. My son was, and still is, not the type of person to accept the fate of the hand that was given to him. Statements like, "You need to face the fact that you may never be able to accomplish the goals you set out for yourself," only added to his determination. Defeat and compromise were not options.

On April 22, we were allowed to bring Ed home for 8 hours and then again on April 23 from 9:30 a.m. to 9:30 p.m. I guess it was a test to see how he'd do without the constant care of the hospital. It was extremely hard having to return him to MFB, but on April 28, he was released as an in-patient and allowed to move back home. Although, for the next six months, he would face the daily routine of returning for out-patient therapy.

Life centered around dropping Ed off in the morning and picking him up later in the afternoon. I don't remember much about this part of the journey, nor do I know exactly what the therapists put him through. I do know their goal was to bring him to a point where he could negotiate normal life. That meant taking him on various "field" trips to malls, stores, high traffic areas, and the like to get him accustomed to noises and interaction with other people. Eventually, they would get him back behind the wheel of a car and help him face the mental trauma concerning this challenge. By the time he returned home each day, his computer brain had shut down totally. Sleep was his only salvation.

MFB also helped him learn how to negotiate living with crutches, something that would become a part of his life for quite some time. Stairs were a big thing. Ed, being so independent, insisted on doing everything himself, without any help from us. Living in a two-story A-frame, it was hard to keep from thinking of him falling and further hurting himself. He became an expert. If something didn't work for him, he'd find another way to make it work. That, pretty much describes Ed. Never accept defeat. Always find a way to make it work. Even then, he was an engineer and a very determined young man. I look back with such pride in my heart for where he came from and what he went through to bring him to where he is today.

May 21 was another milestone. He was allowed to graduate with his class with the stipulation that he'd finish his classes that summer with the help of MFB—a milestone, yes, because there were many moments where this seemed like an impossible dream. It was a long walk from the school to the football field where graduation exercises were to take place. In my mind, I can still see him walking with his fellow classmates, crutches and all, till he reached the podium. It was a very proud moment. In many ways, I think it was good for Ed to leisurely have the summer to finish his classes. As mentally challenging as it was for him, it would help to pave the way for future, harder classes he would have to overcome in the months ahead.

Ed's journey through life has certainly not been an easy one. He's faced adversity and hardship head on. He not only graduated from Embry-Riddle university with a BA in electrical engineering, but eventually went on to receive his master's degree in aeronautical science with a 4.0 GPA. This is my son! This was his journey...the struggles, the hardships, the tears, the joys, the journey. I'm so very proud of him, not simply because of his accomplishments, but because I know what he had to overcome to become the man he is today.

On June 18, 1989, his good friends who he lived with in Florida came to visit. They stayed at our house for over a week. To this day, Ed has no recollection of their visit. Surprising? Yes. But that merely shows the tangible evidence of the long-term effects of a closed head injury. Looking back at all the classes he took and the details he had to remember, you can get just a glimpse of his determination to rise above the obstacles and challenges that faced him on a daily basis.

I am thankful for this time of reflection and for closure for the last 23 years of silence. It hasn't been easy. Reliving is hard. But this journey cannot be complete without giving thanks and praise to God, not just for saving my son's life, but for walking side by side with him throughout every circumstance, every hardship, and every challenge of his life.

There is no doubt in my mind that Ed should've died at the scene of the accident. In talking later to medics who were there, they didn't expect him to live. His heart had stopped. But God had a plan, and maybe part of this plan is for him to help someone, somewhere who is facing similar circumstances.

Quite possibly, someone has given up hope on life as they knew it. Perhaps the words spoken over them have been words of defeat, hopelessness, discouragement, or death. There is no guarantee that your journey will be easy, but God has a plan for your life. He is not responsible for the sudden detours, but He is there to walk with you, side by side, on your journey through this life, regardless of your present situation.

I always told my kids to aim high...aim for the moon. You may not reach it, but you just might grab a star along the way. Ed is living proof of that.

A Father's Perspective

David Meek

Forgive me for bragging, but my one and only son has achieved the career that his dad could only dream about. I may have influenced some of his choices, but unlike me, he not only "Dared to Dream," but was truly "Determined to Do." I am so very proud of his inspiring accomplishments in spite of a huge obstacle that fell into his path.

The year was 1989, and Ed's high school graduation grew near. Ed was growing impatient to move on to the much more interesting engineering classes that college could offer—the classes that would take him into his chosen career.

But then came that fateful evening, an evening that was almost exactly a year after his little sister was injured in a rollover accident and an accident that took the life of one of the three other teenagers in that car with her!

It was Tuesday evening, April 4, 1989, at about 6:10 PM, according to my journal of that year. I was home from work and puttering around as usual. Ed caught up with me and informed me that he was having some trouble with his little car. Without hesitation, I tossed him the keys to our big pickup truck. I didn't want to chance him being stranded late at night on that dark country road. Even though Ed was young then, he had already impressed his dad as being a very careful driver.

A very short while later, we heard sirens. It was all too common to hear sirens up by those crossroads back then. It wasn't long after Ed's accident that the intersection was re-engineered and sirens up there became rare.

Ed's mother and I became nervous when we heard the sirens that night. Then, when we heard the medevac helicopter pass right over our house, his mom went ballistic! I rushed down the stairs behind her, trying to calm her, but she was taking three steps to my two. By that time, the sheriff's car was in the driveway.

The sheriff told us the medevac helicopter was headed for the big hospital downtown, and we hopped in our car to get there as fast as we could. The trip from our house to the hospital usually takes 40 minutes. We made it in 20 minutes.

But once we rushed into the hospital, it was a hurry up and wait and wait and wait and wait! It felt like forever and ever, but eventually news trickled down that Ed was still ALIVE, and they were working on him. As small a piece of news as that might seem, it brought relief and hope to his family. It was truly a miracle!

You can't imagine how BIG and beautiful a miracle was revealed a little later when I got an opportunity to see what was left of our full-size pickup truck. I distinctly remember saying, "Oh my God! Thank You!" If, by another miracle, someone could get that pile of scrap to move, it would only be able to turn in a very small circle since the heavy frame had been bent into a U shape. The center of impact was the driver side door. That was, of course, exactly where Ed had been sitting when the truck hit him.

Our neighbors living close to that intersection said that it looked at first like nobody could have survived in there. The bed of our pickup truck had been thrown clear across the road. The ambulance crews at the accident said they had to use the "jaws of life" just to get near Ed and again to extract him. One of them said that Ed looked so bad that he doubted Ed would even make it to the hospital, so they called for the medivac helicopter to fly him out.

But for me, it was enough that evening just to know he was alive. Alive meant there was hope and the promise of possibilities. There were lots of hurdles to clear. Multiple operations on his neck vertebrae, pelvis, and leg would be required. A steel rod and pins would need to be inserted to help hold his leg together. The physical issues were bad. But we were told that they would heal in time. However, the damage to the brain caused by such a severe crash like Ed was in was an entirely different matter. The brain does not heal like the rest of the body does.

It was quite a while later that evening when we first got to see Ed in the Intensive Care Unit for a few minutes. It was distressing to see him hooked up to all those tubes, the IV's, the oxygen, the neck brace, and the monitors.

Ed gave little indication of being awake or aware of his surroundings. That was to be expected, with the high levels of his medication they had given him. But what a relief to see him. He looked good—for a person that had been through a major car accident. Ignoring the fresh bruises, bumps, and stitches that would eventually go away, we still had our handsome son with us. Yet another wonderful blessing that day to be very thankful for.

Two days after the accident, when the doctors felt he was stable enough, Ed went through 7 hours of surgeries to deal with the severe physical damages. Physically, healing was slow. Progress was very gradual and hard physically. He went from intensive care to a private room after a few days. After about three weeks, Ed was transferred to a specialized rehabilitation hospital in the area.

The Rehab-Hospital continued the physical and mental help and training and retraining that was vitally needed at that point. Physically, wheelchair training came first, and that was followed by crutches when he regained enough strength and coordination. Coordination was the big one, because the brain is critical in any body movements. The accident had damaged muscle-control memory. People are generally so young when they learn these skills that, most of the time, a person may not actually remember ever learning them at all. Imagine being 18 years old and having to relearn the simplest of skills—when even picking up your fork would seem an accomplishment.

To these challenges, add a brain confused by a jumble of incomplete pieces of past and even present events and thoughts. When he opened his clear blue eyes, way back then, he was there physically, but it was strange the way it felt to me. Often, he seemed only partly there. If you approached him suddenly, spoke a little fast, or talked too much, you would lose him mentally, and his eyes would droop and close. We are talking simple, friendly, loving, low key conversions here. But even that type could be an overload for Ed at that time. The many questions of, "Why am I...? Why don't I...? How can I...?", were answered ever so slowly as the mental fog took its time clearing over the months that followed.

There is a strength that comes from adversity, and for Ed, this was his turning point. While fighting his way back through the hurdles and road blocks that were in his way, he gained mental strength and resolve. As he slowly, painstakingly pulled himself back together, he noted that the fields of interest he once had before the accident, those that once caused his mind and imagination to soar, still did. Thinking of these and aiming at his "ultimate goal," he joined the ranks of illustrious others that dared to dream and, in time, live the dream!

Possibly, that is the reason why more than a few of the closed head injury "recoveries" go on to attain goals that other individuals don't. Undoubtedly, they gain a deeper understanding of their brain and a greater sense of what it is really capable of.

A Sister's Perspective

Wendi DeYoung

I am the sister of a rocket scientist. This is not always an easy thing. You can imagine some of the questions I am asked. A typical conversation may go like this:

"So, how many brothers and sisters do you have?" someone may ask.

"Just one brother," I'd reply.

"Really, and what does he do?"

"Oh, he's a rocket scientist."

"What? Wow! And uh, what is it that you do?"

At that point, I could tell them that I owned my own business, or was a successful author, or even that I invented the wheel. It doesn't matter. After they hear "rocket scientist," the expectations go through the roof and nothing else is quite good enough. It is much the same as if you went to a concert and some famous singer came on stage and put on the show of a lifetime, and then afterward, an unknown singer tried to follow.

"So, what happened to you?" a few have asked me.

"Well, I was the one that got the looks," I say with a chuckle.

Does this irritate me? Does it hurt me to not be able to measure up to what others see my brother as? I can answer that with an enthusiastic no way! My brother Ed is a success story. Ed is a success because of what he went through, but he didn't let it stop him.

God had a plan when Ed was a lost boy looking for direction. He also had a plan when Ed was a teenager dying in the hospital. And God most definitely has a plan now that Ed is a rocket scientist with a life changing testimony.

I have been impacted by Ed's life. And I, the annoying little sister, have come to be his number one fan. I have witnessed, with unfiltered eyes, his transition from death to life. I can look back and see the very hand of God reach down and pluck him up out of the place he was in, shake him up a bit, and put him back down where he needed to be. And all this was done through a devastating and miraculous car accident. It was only at the time of his impending death that his life really began.

Ed was seventeen when God opened his eyes and began to reveal his purpose. Only God knew what it would take for this to happen. In Ed's case, it took near devastation. Often enough, God must take us through a place of loss before we can ever come to a place of surrender. But we have to wonder, what gives? Why does such a loving God allow us to arrive at such a place? Why does life have to seem so unfair sometimes?

These are questions that all who have traveled this road of devastation have asked. And through Ed's story of redemption, we want to help you walk down this painful road. We have gone before you for a reason, and our paths now connect in order to help give you answers and hope. Our prayer and mission is that it does just that. So, hang on tight. Things aren't always as they seem!

A Wife's Perspective

Christine Meek

I didn't know. Well, he told me he had been in a car accident before and hurt his leg, but he never let me know until recently the extent of his injuries, his recovery, or his fight. When I met him at Central Michigan University, I thought he was smart and cute and kind, and we instantly connected. I remember that first night we met, the light shone down on him and around him, and he was just glowing. I knew right then he was special. We were fast friends.

When I was having a hard time in calculus, he told me he had aced it and could tutor me. I had no idea he had taken it three times. Side by side, we worked through the matrices and formulas that eluded me. Step by small step, he guided me through the confusion that is calculus. I loved those sessions in the quiet of the library and very much looked forward to seeing him each week.

After an especially tough study session, we'd head over to a relaxation room—a soundproof study room that piped in soft, relaxing music. We'd chat, and his eyes would get heavy. "I need to rest just a few minutes," he'd say timidly, a little embarrassed maybe. Resting his head in my lap, he'd nap for a while, and I would dream of a possible future with my good friend, Ed. That happened a lot, his getting sleepy.

I'm a high energy, a let's *go* kind of girl. I loved hiking, canoeing, swimming—go, go, go. When we weren't trying to make adventures, he studied. A lot! He pushed himself so hard physically and mentally that there were many times his brain would just shut down. He spent a lot of time in that relaxation room as the music was soothing and the privacy allowed for him to lay his head down and close his eyes.

I met Ed less than four years after his accident. During those previous four years, Ed fought all the time. He fought the pain in his body. He fought the doctors and specialists that told him he shouldn't/couldn't go to school. He fought the sadness and doubt that would creep in his mind. He fought hard for four years. So, by the time I met him, he was starting to get tired.

Fighting that hard for that long is exhausting. He saw in me a renewed sense of strength and purpose, and he now had a partner to fight alongside him. He leaned on me a lot to motivate him and help him organize his space and time. And I leaned on him too. His friendship and love were abundant and still are. On my bad days, he lets me put my head in his lap and caresses me while telling me how strong I am and how much he believes in me. And I get to remind him of his strength and resiliency when he needs it.

Back then, I had no real idea of just how strong he really was. I took for granted how hard he had to work to keep up in his classes. They were pre-engineering classes, so I knew they were hard. There's a reason that most people choose a general liberal art class over calculus 3. But Ed pushed himself! While sitting in class, he had a hard time staying awake or being able to listen to the lecture *and* take notes at the same time. The solution, he found, was at Radio Shack.

A cheap little audio recorder saved the day. At the beginning of class, he'd hit record, then sit in class and just try to pay attention, just try to stay awake. He had no worry about taking notes, no worry about what he might be missing. He could be fully engaged. At the end of class, he'd frantically write down all the he could remember and then go back home or to the relaxation room and take a nap.

Later, he'd listen to that recording, look at the notes he'd written down at the end of class, and get a full view of what had happened. In essence, it took Ed twice as long as everyone else to get through a semester since he took every class twice.

In some of our conversations, I would ask him when he thought he was going to graduate, but he was never able to give me a straight answer. That annoyed me since I knew every class I was going to take every semester until I graduated. I'm a bit neurotic like that and have a need to control as much of my environment as possible. Ed just took things one semester at a time. I knew he had big goals, but his apparent lackadaisical attitude toward getting there bothered me. He had a list of classes that he had to take before graduation, but he had no idea when he'd take those classes. "Taking it as it comes" was a way of life for him. It was planned spontaneity if you will. That challenged me in a big way!

Perfectionism, striving to be or at least look like 100%, was a huge goal for me. And if I knew I wasn't going to be perfect, I never even wanted to try. Not at my perfect weight? I'll just eat another candy bar instead of working out. Not getting the A in the class I wanted? Turning in this homework won't make a difference then. Don't have the "perfect" dress to wear? Why bother even going out. The mental block I had of understanding that "done" was better than "perfect" stopped me from pursuing some pretty amazing opportunities.

But Ed, he was different. He just went for it, good, bad, or indifferent—even if he thought, even if he *knew*, that he wasn't going to get an A or look his best. He would still go for it. He always tries his best, regardless of a perfect or not so perfect outcome. Watching him step into the unknown is so inspiring.

May in Mt. Pleasant, Michigan, brings trees budding, flowers blooming, and birds singing the praises of springtime at last! In 1996, it also brought graduation for me. Ed still had a ways to go, but we were ready to get married. We had the perfect wedding—the elegant white dress, tuxedos with coat tails, the scent of fresh flowers filling the sanctuary, and 250 encouraging and loving guests to send us on the beginning of our lifelong adventure. It was a fairytale come true. Ed was so handsome and loving, and it felt like nothing would ever stop this feeling.

And then we moved.

We moved 1,900 miles across the United States to get Ed to the college of his dreams: Embry-Riddle Aeronautical University. I got him to commit to putting on paper the true plan of finishing his degree: two years and he'd be done. I would work to support us through that endeavor so that he could concentrate on the rigors of the electrical engineering program.

In the small town of Prescott, Arizona, there weren't a lot of places to work. Walmart was the largest employer at the time. No thanks. Luckily, Ed had saved up a good amount of money to get us started until I finally found a job at a historic hotel in the sales department.

While I worked 9 to 5, Ed was at school studying. He'd drop me off, go to school, pick me up, we'd have dinner, and then he'd head back to school. Guess who made dinner? Guess who did the laundry? Guess who changed the oil on the car? Ed was so engrossed in getting through all his difficult classes that it lay on my shoulders to do everything else. I wanted to be the perfect wife. Images of Donna Reed in the movie *It's a Wonderful Life* come to mind. Well dressed, with dinner on the stove, the light shining through my perfectly coiffed hair—well…that was the image I had in my mind, but it was not reality. Not even close.

Our laundry room was the closet in the kitchen next to the dinner table. Towels, shirts, and socks piled up on the table waiting to be folded and put away. After working all day, I tried to juggle making dinner and doing laundry at the same time. Instead of doing it all "perfectly," the smell of fresh laundry mixed with the pungent odor of burning pasta. Ed would come home, fix himself a sandwich, and push the laundry to the other side of the table so he could sit and eat. He didn't fix me a sandwich or help to fold anything. He just sat, gazing blankly into nothingness and chewed.

It might seem like this was insensitive or thoughtless of him, and you'd be right. He was not sensitive and neither did he take much thought about all the laundry or the work that needed to be done *because he didn't see it.* It never occurred to him all that was unraveling because his mind only had enough space to handle the school work that he had on his plate.

On the weekends, I would chuck all responsibility so we could head out to the mountains for a hike or campout and have some fun. I needed a break from reality, and Ed needed a break from thinking. On road trips, when Ed gets sleepy or the sun starts to set, I always drive. The fading light plays tricks on him, and he never will fully trust that a truck won't come out of nowhere and hit him again. Sunday nights came, and we'd head home to be met by the laundry that was still on the table and the burnt pan which still lay in the sink, beckoning me to scrub it. Sunday nights were the hardest.

It wasn't Ed's fault. I took on the responsibility of all the house chores in addition to working full time and starting a business for a reason. I made sure he didn't get distracted by the demands of the car or the bills or the cat so that he could succeed at school. I worked so hard to build an environment that would allow him to focus on the goal of graduation.

And, day after day, he too worked hard. Blurry eyed, we'd crawl out of bed, start the coffee, hop in the car to start the day long ritual of work for me and school for him. I'd fall into bed at night with the glow of the desk lamp letting me know that Ed wasn't quite ready to fall into a slumber. It was over 10 years later that I learned about how truly devastating his accident really was and how the brain injury affected everything.

It took him 9 years total, from his first class after the accident until 2 years into our marriage, but he graduated! Not with honors, but he did it. He succeeded at the one thing doctors told him he'd probably never do: finish school and become an engineer. He overcame so much, and we sacrificed so much to attain this goal. And he made me know that his diploma was as much my success as his since I set up the lifestyle that allowed him to solely focus on school. He even gave me a "retirement" party and told me I never had to work again if I didn't want to. And we moved 1,900 miles back to Michigan to start our family and our new life.

I spent the first two years of our marriage creating a bubble for Ed. If I hadn't, and he had to pitch in with dishes or cleaning, and he'd end up having to take a nap after each chore or sleep all day Saturday. He just didn't have the stamina to concentrate on the "little things." This continued after he got a job, and it was a pattern we held for years, because healing from a traumatic brain injury doesn't happen quickly.

I could tell something wasn't right. The alarm yelled, "Good morning!", but Ed had a hard time getting out of bed every day. He moseyed his way out the door and headed to work, and then he'd fall into bed at the end of the night completely crushed by the day's activity. There was no fever, no sickness, but Ed was having a hard time adjusting to the constant demands of his new job, and on top of that, he hated it. I saw it in his eyes. All the energy he spent trying to make work-life be productive left him with little or nothing to give when he got home.

Although I wasn't working outside the house now, we had a new baby, and I was still trying to create the "perfect" environment for Ed. I got to try to be that perfect Donna Reed housewife, but became inundated by the ridiculous pressure I put on myself to hold that standard. I was fulltime mom to a colicky baby, doing all the cooking and cleaning (all perfect Donna Reed stuff), but I also did all the painting, grass mowing, oil changing, and snow shoveling. Ed still needed me to create an environment that would allow him to focus all his energy on making it through the work day and just come home and relax at night.

I started to unravel and burn out. I stopped cooking and just bought frozen pizzas for dinner. I stopped trying to put the laundry away, and it started to pile up on the dryer. We called that mound Mt. Washmore. I dropped the vision of the perfect "Donna Reed" way of life and just did what I could. Dishes stayed in the sink or on the table, the sticky floor attracted dust and crumbs like a magnet, and grass clippings sat in small piles on the lawn. These visual reminders constantly shouted at me of all I didn't do, couldn't do, or wouldn't do.

I spent my time playing with my son rather than cleaning. Sitting down with Ed and a couple of glasses of wine held precedence over weeding the yard. On the weekends, rather than enlist Ed's help with chores, we would escape on a road trip and forget our struggles while sitting around a campfire, roasting marshmallows. But Sunday night always came to show us the piled-up laundry, the unvacuumed floors, the dirty sinks.

Ed never "saw" the mess. It wasn't that he was just ignoring it or pretending not to see it to make me feel better, he literally didn't see the chaos that was our home. I had to let go of any dreams of a clean, tidy house if I wanted to maintain my sanity. As soon as I dropped my idea of perfection, things went more smoothly in the Meek household. But really, all Ed needed was for me to make a list or to tell him exactly what I needed him to do. He wasn't just being lazy, he just didn't see anything wrong with the way we were living. And I didn't hold him accountable.

Ed hated that first job out of college. I thought it was because he was putting in 12 plus hour days and that it was really hard. I found out later that the reason he would leave at 8:30 a.m. and come home around 9 p.m. was because he took over a two-hour lunch to go to a restaurant or out to a movie. The doldrum of being trapped in a cubicle where people never smiled or talked or shared ideas was so stifling for Ed. I knew that, in order for him to stay sane, he needed to work for a company that would allow him to work with a real team, to share his ideas, and to be in a location with blue skies.

Ready as always to support him through anything, I suggested that Ed look for another job—somewhere where there was sun (it certainly wasn't in western Michigan) and a better work culture. He contacted a colleague in New Mexico, and four weeks later, he headed out to prepare the way for us to follow.

It was three months before I got to see him again. During that time, Ed had to figure out a way to feed himself, cleanup after himself, and keep the car running all while trying to learn a new job, in a new city, by himself. It wasn't perfect, but he did it. When push comes to shove, Ed can do it! But when we came back together, he was so tired. He saw me as respite and, fast as lightning, we reverted to the roles we had established at the beginning of our marriage: he just focused on his job and I took care of everything else. He leaned on me so much. He counted on my ability to go, go, go and to take care of just about everything. I was his rock, and he always let me know it.

I am the luckiest married woman ever. Ed is forever telling me how beautiful I am or how much he appreciates all I do. He constantly reminds me that he couldn't do "this" without me. It's hard, sometimes, to be mad at his lack of contribution around the house when he holds me in his arms at night, stroking my hair, and telling me how much he loves me.

On Saturdays, when he sleeps until 11 or 12 and the babies have been up for over six hours and I haven't showered or had a chance to eat, I start to get really resentful. When he finally drags himself out of bed, lumbers over to me to give me a huge hug, and says, "Thank you," I almost forget how tired I am. I kiss him and tell him I love him as I hand the baby over to him and finally go take a shower.

Eighteen months after our first son was born, we welcomed a second into our lives. Our family was now complete. And, oh my, does Ed loves his boys! He loves them deeply, but it's hard having two babies to care for at once.

Ed would come home from a long day at work and just want to rest and unwind. Babies and toddlers and young children will never let you do that, however! They are loud and demanding and curious. Even after more than 10 years after his accident, he still had evidence of a brain injury. He could lose focus still, he was quick to lose his temper, and he had a hard time keeping organized. (Please, oh please do not look on his side of the bed!)

I know when Ed has had a hard day and was struggling to focus when he stands in front of the TV with his fingers clutched around his coffee mug and he forgets to take a sip. It was on those kinds of days that I tried to keep the kids quiet so that Ed wouldn't get overwhelmed at home on top of what he was going through at work. Video games to the rescue. Ed somehow managed to convince our boys that it was fun to sit and watch Daddy play games on the television.

The three of them would sit as Ed took the control while the boys directed him on what to do and where to go. "Get the bad guy, Daddy," they would shout. Ed figured out a way to connect with his children that still allowed him to relax after work by playing "Daddy games." He was never the dad that threw the ball with them or went on bike rides or things like that. Those activities took too much energy and stamina, neither of which he ever had. But they all loved sitting around, cheering him on as he beat the Big Boss dude.

When Ed told me that his work would pay for him to get his master's degree, I knew that meant a couple of things. First, having a master's degree was a big deal to forward his career. Second, we were still paying off student loans from his bachelor's degree. It was a huge blessing to have his work foot the bill. We couldn't pass that up. Third, if he went for his master's degree and continued to work, there was no way he'd have any energy left over for anything...not even Daddy games.

Ed would go to work, head straight to class, come home to eat and then to study, and then go to bed. He was completely blind to anything outside of his narrow focus unless it was really loud. Ed can't handle loud noises; it hurts his head and makes him extremely jumpy. If the boys got too rowdy, he would yell for them to be quiet. He was maxed out when it came to concentration and self-control. Those two years were tougher than when he went through his bachelor's program. But he made it; *we* made it. When they called his name during the graduation ceremony, we were the obnoxious, excited, proud, cheering section for him.

We moved a lot to help get Ed's career take off, literally, into space—Arizona, Michigan, New Mexico, Colorado, and West Virginia. Who knew that there was a NASA facility in Fairmont, WV? Pride, excitement, and an overwhelming sense of accomplishment was on Ed's face and in his heart when he got his NASA badge and NASA email address. But that was the one move that broke me.

I was so tired and felt so lost with yet another cross-country move. We had lived in thirteen places by that point, and the new house was a 100-year-old farmhouse that needed a *lot* of work. I no longer had the energy or inner drive to do all the things that needed to be done. But Ed stepped up! He was able to do his job during the day *and* come home and help me do projects around the house.

In less than three years, we remodeled two bathrooms, the kitchen, painted forty-five gallons of paint, tore out carpeting, refinished original hardwood floors, and replaced window panes. There was so much we did together. I was at the end of my rope after seventeen years of setting up plans, helping Ed with routines, doing all the work around the house, and making life easy for him when he got home from work.

And when I broke, he was there for me. He was now able to pick up *my* pieces and help create a space for *me* to recover. He no longer slept until noon on Saturdays, but rather he fixed the fence or worked on the water heater. He no longer spent hours playing video games or watching TV when coming home from work, but rather he helped me get dinner ready. I had to completely lean on him for support and encouragement just like he had been leaning on me for the previous 17 years.

We made our way back to Colorado where we are happier and more relaxed than we've ever been in our entire relationship. Although his leg doesn't hurt like it used to, it still makes a good weather indicator to know when the rain will come. He can focus longer too. His side of the bed is still a mess, and I wonder if that was a brain injury issue or if he is just genetically predisposed to being a slob. He does still lose his temper, and we get into acute arguments pretty quickly. But they aren't long lasting so long as we forgive quickly and forget even faster.

Ed will never be fully cured of his brain injury, but he has made *tremendous* progress from where he was when I met him. To think about all the challenges he went through, that *we* went through, to get here is nothing less than a miracle. Ed is a miracle.

Ed and I make an amazing team. We are best friends and have the utmost respect for each other. Having a plan, a lot of prayer, leaning on each other, and a lot of practice is what kept us going during the hard times. Those are the strategies we used to enjoy the good times too.

I am so proud of him, of us. I thank God for all the steps that led us to where we are now. It certainly wasn't easy and, I may have been crazy at times for sticking with him, but it was worth it!

I love you, Ed.

If you would like your group, corporation, or event to hear Ed's inspiring story of triumph over tragedy, of how to stay on track with your goals, and the key to fulfilling your life's dreams go to:
www.ERtotheStars.com/speaker.html.